Praise for *The Zen of Social Media Marketing*

"*The Zen of Social Media Marketing* demystifies the wacky, yet immensely powerful new world of online conversational marketing and serves as a great primer to understand where to allocate your time, money, and energy. A great read for entrepreneurs, professionals, and small business."

—JONATHAN FIELDS, Author of *Career Renegade*

"Building on a strong background of expert marketing advice, Shama has again produced a body of work that is at once complete and practical. This is a book that you can read quickly when you're frustrated by what seems like endless contradictions of social media, and then referenced again and again as you develop your own sense of place on the social web. It is, after all, quite correctly titled *The Zen of Social Media Marketing*. I highly recommend this book."

—DAVE EVANS, Social Media Strategist,
and Author of *Social Media Marketing: An Hour a Day*

"Shama breaks down the 'why' and 'how' with easy-to-understand examples that can get you on the right track immediately...and ultimately grow your business."

—JOE PULIZZI, Co-Author of *Get Content. Get Customers*,
and Founder of Junta42

"Finally! A true authority on the subject of social media has broken through the utter noise of get-rich-quick-with-social-media hysteria. Shama takes the mystery and hype out of social media and gives readers a practical step-by-step action plan to start, grow, measure, expand, and optimize their online presence. It is a must-read for any marketing professional, C-level executive, or entrepreneur. Her conversational writing style, numerous case studies, and 'how-to' guides with screen shots make learning and implementing almost elementary. It will be *required reading* for all our clients."

—JOE ABRAHAM, Founder and Managing Director at En Corpus Group, and Author of *B.O.S.I. Entrepreneurship*

"Ready for a *true* social marketing awakening? If so, be sure and take Shama Kabani's *The Zen of Social Media Marketing* on your path to web enlightenment."

—DEAN LINDSAY, Author of *The Progress Challenge* and *Cracking the Networking CODE*

"*The Zen of Social Media Marketing* is a comprehensive guide for maximizing the marketing opportunities from online networks. Shama Kabani helps you make the most of your efforts in marketing through a stronger knowledge of social media."

—PENELOPE TRUNK, Founder of the Social Network Brazen Careerist

---

"Shama is hands-down the industry leader in social media marketing and creating buzz. She has a rare combination of social media savvy and law-of-attraction mastery that businesses clamor to find. It's easy to see why she's called the 'Shaman of social media.' She will transform your marketing and increase your sales. Listen to everything this luminary says."

—SHAWNE DUPERON, Five-Time EMMY® Award Winner, ShawneTV

"*The Zen of Social Media Marketing* is for anyone that has ever felt overwhelmed by all of the online options available now for networking, socializing, and just plain being online in general! Shama breaks it down so that even the most social media–phobes will be breathing sighs of relief at how simple she makes it all sound! Get this book today and be on your way to a stress-free online experience that you will groove and align with, thrive, and enjoy."

—SALLY SHIELDS, Author of *The DIL Rules*

The Zen of Social Media MARKETING

An Easier Way to Build Credibility,
Generate Buzz, and Increase Revenue

....

Shama Hyder Kabani

BENBELLA BOOKS, INC.

DALLAS, TEXAS

BenBella Books, Inc.
10300 N. Central Expressway, Suite 400
Dallas, TX 75231
www.benbellabooks.com
Send feedback to feedback@benbellabooks.com

Printed in the United States of America
10 9 8 7 6 5 4

Library of Congress Cataloging-in-Publication data is available for this title.
ISBN 978-1-935251-73-6

Copyediting by Rebecca Logan
Proofreading by Erica Lovett and Gregory Teague
Cover design by Faceout Studio, Tim Green
Text design and composition by John Reinhardt Book Design
Printed by Bang Printing

Distributed by Perseus Distribution
http://www.perseusdistribution.com/

To place orders through Perseus Distribution:
Tel: (800) 343-4499
Fax: (800) 351-5073
E-mail: orderentry@perseusbooks.com

Significant discounts for bulk sales are available.
Please contact Glenn Yeffeth at glenn@benbellabooks.com or (214) 750-3628.

Contents

Acknowledgments

Arshil Kabani (my husband)—Thank you for always dreaming big for me. I couldn't do what I do without you. I love you.

Javeed and Suraiya Hyder (my parents)—Thank you for your constant support and love. I am truly blessed to have you as my parents. I couldn't imagine being more loved. I am who I am today because of you.

Sofiya Hyder (my sister)—Thank you for always standing by my side. Your generosity is unparalleled.

Aziz and Nargis Kabani (my in-laws)—Thank you for raising Arshil the way you did. And thank you for treating me like the daughter you never had. I couldn't do this without your support.

Dawna Ballard (professor)—Thank you for being the ultimate example of a classy professional woman. I aspire to be more like you every day.

Michael Seeley (teacher)—Thank you for igniting my passion for technology. Your patience and compassion have always moved me.

Janet Goldstein (my agent)—Thank you for believing in me and in this book. It could not have been made possible without you.

Leah Wilson (editor, BenBella)—Thank you for your encouragement and keen eye. Your editing has made this book what it is today.

Glenn Yeffeth (publisher, BenBella)—Thank you for your immense support. May all authors be as lucky as I am to have a publisher like you!

Stephanie Cross (my right hand!)—Thank you for your unwavering loyalty and hard work. Thank you for reminding me that we are blessed, not stressed.

My clients—Thank you for allowing me to guide you online. Thank you for your trust, your respect, and your belief in me.

Entire team at The Marketing Zen Group (formerly Click To Client)—Thank you for being the strength behind my work. You guys are so talented and hardworking. I am constantly impressed.

Snoopy and Maui (my dog and cat)—Thank you for being the office mascots and for letting me bounce ideas off you—even if it was during a game of fetch.

Foreword

Shama Kabani starts off her book with a scene from *The Matrix*. I know the scene well. It's a little bit of philosophy thrown into Hollywood and made simple to consume. Shama's right for giving us this gem; *The Matrix* seems to have motivated a lot of us to think differently about how we live online, and how business works.

I know. I wrote about *The Matrix* a few different times in *Trust Agents*. We could have just written, "To be a trust agent is to know how to be Neo," and it would've been a shorter book.

There is a zen to social media. There is a way. Shama's right about that. And her way—her thoughts, her experiments, her recommendations in this book—is one that can get a lot of people closer to the prize than anything they might intuit and do on their own.

Business rules are different now. Don't believe me? How are the banks in the United States doing? How are the three big car makers? How are small businesses doing? You want to keep marketing the way companies have been for the last fifty years? Not a good idea, I'm afraid.

We're writing new code, and Shama knows it.

There's human code out there all about how human you can be, how you can connect with people, and what that means for business. I'm flying all over the planet right now writing new versions of this code for companies, showing them how to be human. The goal is simple: explain to people that, while face-to-face is just as important as it ever was, now we've got all kinds of new tools that let us tighten bonds in between those in-person moments.

These tools leave a wake of data behind them. Follow these invisible trails of data and you can smell new customers, new opportunities. New networks don't form inside your inbox. New phone numbers don't start following you (frankly, that's probably a good thing). Social media provides the links and connections that allow these networks to form. I've taken to calling Twitter the Serendipity Engine, because that's what it harnesses: serendipity. And you, too, can harness it for your business.

Shama has a way of teaching this new code—her business-savvy Zen approach—that fits the business you're in, the person you are, and the results you want. I might do a few things differently, but we all might. (After all, if you see Buddha on the road, kill him. Isn't that the quote?) And you need to consider what parts of her approach you'll benefit most from implementing. But ignoring her isn't a good move.

Get into *The Zen of Social Media Marketing*. Keep a notepad file hand. Write down notes. Seek out everything that makes sense for you. Start setting up some next moves based on what you learn. Shama will show you.

Meanwhile, I'm waiting for the white rabbit.

—Chris Brogan,
Co-author of *The New York Times*
and *Wall Street Journal* bestseller *Trust Agents*

A Note to the Reader

Dearest Reader,

This may be the first book of its kind: the first official "living" book on social media. What this means is that I've posted a mirror copy of this book online at www.ZenofSocialMedia.com. (You can access it using the passphrase "thank you.") Social media itself is a living, evolving thing, and the digital copy of *The Zen of Social Media Marketing* will be updated regularly to reflect changes as they occur, making it the last social media guide you'll ever need. The book you hold in your hands is your key to accessing that digital copy and more.

There are two ways to use this book, and how you choose depends on your style and personal preference.

1. You can read it from cover to cover and walk away with a solid understanding of social media and how to be a Zen-like social media marketer.

or

2. You can use it as a guide and create your own social media strategy as you read. There is a workbook that accompanies this book, and you can find that and much more guidance at www.ZenofSocialMedia.com.

Either way you choose to proceed, my sincerest intention is for you to walk away with a thorough understanding of how to succeed using social media.

Thank you for picking up this book. Thank you for wanting to learn more about this new online world. And, most of all, thank you for trusting me to be your guide.

Your #1 fan,
Shama Hyder Kabani

Introduction

Why Write This?

It was about six in the evening, and I had wrapped up my work for the day and was heading out the door when my phone rang. It was a woman, a business consultant, and she was clearly upset. It sounded like she was on the verge of tears, so I put down my things and asked if I could help her. Her response was an emotionally charged monologue filled with frustration and disappointment. *"They banned my account from Facebook...I don't even know what I did wrong. I just don't GET social media. I hear about people who are very successful using it, but I don't know where to start. How do I even BEGIN to catch up? I have fifteen followers on Twitter...others have thousands! I am a successful consultant! I run a seven-figure business, yet I can't help but feel like I am missing out on a key component in my marketing!"*

I sympathized with her, but I realized that she wasn't alone. I'm used to getting calls and emails from frustrated business owners and marketers who struggle to make sense of social media. As one man put it, "It's like swimming upstream!"

That's how the idea for this book was born.

One day, it just *clicked!* I realized the main reason people are struggling with social media marketing: they are going against the natural order of things! The traditional marketing rules cannot be applied to social media because social media is not a marketer's platform. It belongs to consumers.

For the longest time, marketing consisted of putting out a message about a business or product that was controlled strictly by the business itself. Think about a square peg. The square peg represents the traditional marketing message. Now, imagine square holes. Each hole is a traditional marketing medium—print, radio, and television. The square peg fits the square hole perfectly.

However, here comes social media: multiple online mediums all controlled by the people participating within them—people who are busy having conversations, sharing resources, and forming their own communities. Social media is full of constant activity controlled by no one individual in particular. Unlike radio, television, and print, it isn't passive: Users don't just receive content; they create it, too. Social media is a circular hole. Yet most marketers are still using a square peg. They are working *against* the grain. And they're finding themselves thoroughly stumped and no better off than they were when they started on their journey.

I wanted something I could hand to these frustrated folks, something that could help social media make *sense* to them. **I wanted something that would finally help marketers understand how to utilize social media marketing concepts in a practical and efficient manner. I wanted to help them find the circular peg to fit the circular hole.**

I wanted to show them the *Zen* of social media marketing. Once you truly understand how social media functions, marketing using social media channels becomes effortless.

The Zen of What?

Yes, I know. Spending hours on social media sites only to be disappointed by a zero return on your investment doesn't put you in a Zen-like state. But that happens *only* if you are doing it wrong! If you go with the flow, you can rake in the profits *and* have fun. Imagine that!

The Zen of social media marketing is about understanding the mind-set of people who are using social media and then using it to your advantage.

Do you remember the famous scene from *The Matrix* where Neo bends the spoon? It went like this:

SPOON BOY: Do not try and bend the spoon. That's impossible. Instead...only try to realize the truth.

NEO: What truth?

SPOON BOY: There is no spoon.

NEO: There is no spoon?

SPOON BOY: Then you'll see that it is not the spoon that bends; it is only yourself.

Social media is like that spoon. If you try to bend it, it won't bend. If, instead, you bend—if you alter your own attitude and how you market—you win. Have you ever wondered how some people rack up friends and followers, cultivate fans, and just seem to be *everywhere* at once? These people are true Zen marketers. They may not even realize they're doing anything special; they just go with the flow. They make it look effortless because so much of it *is* effortless.

Now, if you are thinking this book is just going to tell you to breathe deeply and use the force, think again. Like every good Zen master, you need some tools in your arsenal. In the following pages, I will share with you all the tools and techniques you need to become the ideal social media marketer—the guy or gal people want to be friends with and whose business gets talked about constantly.

A Personal Story

I launched my online marketing business right out of graduate school, on my own with no resources, in August of 2007. By August 2008, I had built it into a firm with employees and clients around the world. And 100 percent of our clients came to us from our online marketing efforts, specifically our social media marketing efforts. My bootstrapped business had made six figures in less than a year.

I continued to hire the best people to help grow our team until we became a truly full-service web agency. Whatever our clients needed online, we could provide. Soon, the business fueled its own growth. Word spread quickly; that's the nature of online marketing! I started receiving invitations to speak at top industry conferences, earned interviews with television media, and had to start turning away more clients than I was taking on. As the business grew, so did my personal brand. I am humbled by and grateful for our growth.

My company is living proof that, when done right, social media marketing *works* for businesses. And it works, albeit slightly differently, for businesses of all sizes and types. I know this because we have worked with clients at all stages—from start-ups to well-established firms—to leverage social media. **It is my sincerest intention to share with you the same wisdom that helped my company and our clients' companies grow.** Throughout this book, you will find the stories of businesses from a variety of industries that are successfully marketing through social platforms. If they can do it, so can you!

Who Is This Guide a Perfect Fit For?

If you are responsible for marketing in any shape or form, this guide is written for you. Perhaps you are a small business owner responsible for attracting your own customers or clientele, or perhaps you're an employee at a huge firm who is responsible for your company's social media efforts. Maybe you want to get the word out about your nonprofit. It doesn't matter; the principles are all the same. This book will show you exactly how to leverage social media to accomplish your goals.

What *does* matter is that you are

- Committed to marketing or promoting your service/product/blog/organization in an ethical and unassuming manner
- Willing to listen, communicate, and share (the building blocks of social media marketing)
- *Okay* with doing things the easy way and don't insist on going against the grain

Social media marketing does not have to be a struggle.

Who Is This Guide Not a Good Fit For?

This guide is *not* for those who want to become overnight millionaires, internet marketers looking to turn a quick buck, or those looking to grow their Facebook friend count so they can spam those friends. Sorry to disappoint you! The strategies and techniques I lay out in this book are for legitimate businesses that will apply them with consistency and commitment—two necessary elements for social media success.

What Will You Learn?

✓ Where social media marketing fits in the bigger scheme of things
✓ How to make your website or blog the hub of your online marketing efforts
✓ How to use Facebook, Twitter, and LinkedIn for online marketing in an ethical manner
✓ How to drive traffic to your sites
✓ How to build credibility and establish expertise
✓ How to generate leads
✓ How to build your own community of fans
✓ How to build your e-zine/newsletter list
✓ How to measure your social media marketing efforts
✓ How to find and create strategic joint venture relationships using social media
✓ How to leverage your past success to gain future customers and clients
✓ How to get speaking engagements
✓ What you *must* have *before* you start social media marketing
✓ The number one reason people fail at social media marketing and how to avoid that mistake

Case Studies and Profiles

In addition to the case studies peppered throughout the book, you will also find a group of profiles at the end. These profiles present *real* people and businesses using social media marketing to achieve their goals. They aren't all marketers by profession but are marketing and promoting their causes successfully nonetheless.

Here's to you—a future Zen master of social media marketing! Let the journey begin.

Online Marketing Basics

BEFORE WE LOOK AT ONLINE MARKETING, let's look at traditional or offline marketing. This will help set the foundation for marketing on the internet. Before the advent of the internet, there were predominantly three main ways to market. These traditional marketing avenues were print, TV, and radio. Print included newspapers, magazines, yellow pages, posters, billboards, and even direct mail. Radio and TV included commercials and spots or segments. Traditional marketing worked very well for many years for three main reasons.

REASON 1: Marketing was a one-way street. Companies talked at the consumers, and this was expected because there really was no viable way for customers to talk back. Sure, word of mouth existed. However, you would realistically only tell Joe, Sally, and maybe Mary (if she was in town) before moving on. Moreover, it took a long time for word to get around. So, basically, if the nice-looking lady on television said the laundry detergent was amazing, we believed it. Today, we can go on a company's Facebook page, find them on Twitter, or even comment on their blog. Customers can—and are—talking back!

REASON 2: We were all the same, more or less. Let's face it! We wore the same clothes, had the same habits, and enjoyed the same activities. It was easier for marketers to target buyers because they knew exactly who and where they were. Targeting a woman in her thirties? She was most likely a married, mother of two, and a stay-at-home mom. She put her family first and most likely went to church on Sundays. Try targeting a woman in her thirties today. She *may* be a stay-at-home mom to two kids and go to church on Sundays. But she may just as likely be a single woman focused on her career who enjoys hiking on the weekends. Today, you need a multipronged approach. You can't reach a demographic through one channel. You have to reach people through the channel of their choice.

REASON 3: We were less tired—and a little less jaded. At first, we believed the man on television when he said that his product could eliminate any stain. We believed it when the woman who reminded us of Grandma said the cookies tasted freshly baked. We believed it all—for a while. We were so transfixed by the well-written copy in the magazine or the flashy ad on TV. Today, we are a lot savvier. We check reviews, leave comments, and demand trial versions.

Does this mean traditional marketing is over? Not at all. It has, however, evolved. The internet has woven its way through every form of traditional marketing. When was the last time you got a piece of direct mail that didn't have a website address for you to visit? Every morning I listen to NPR (National Public Radio), and every morning the broadcasters invite me to tweet them my questions or fan their Facebook page.

What is online marketing? Online marketing is the art and science (dare I say the Zen?) of leveraging the internet to get your message across so that you can move people to take action. Whether that action is donating their time to your cause or buying your product or service, the goal of marketing has always ˈ same—to get people to take action. The tools just keep c

If online marketing is the act of leveraging the internet in general to get your message across, social media marketing is the act of leveraging specifically social media platforms (places where

> The social media movement has provided the business owner powerful tools for reaching thousands of prospects and clients at the click of a mouse. However, without a strong business strategy and knowledge of online marketing, these tools are often used in vain. Success in this new media requires you to lead with a strong business mind-set.
>
> To that end, ask yourself:
>
> - What exactly am I trying to accomplish with social media and why?
> - What are my readers' most pressing challenges, and how can I help them overcome these?
> - What are the most effective delivery tools for my messages?
> - How can I build enduring relationships and turn strangers into lifetime customers?
>
> **Mitch Meyerson,**
> *author of* Mastering Online Marketing *and eight other books*
> *(www.MitchMeyerson.com)*

people connect and communicate) to promote a product or a service to increase sales.

First I want to share with you a simple framework for marketing online. This framework is necessary because social media marketing is not a stand-alone process or outcome. It is part of the bigger marketing picture. So, before we delve into the specifics, we have to take in the big picture.

Successful online marketing can be broken down into three distinct components. I like to use the acronym "ACT" to describe the process.

The ACT Methodology

CONVERT

Successful
Online
Marketing

ATTRACT

TRANSFORM

A is for Attract. To attract means to get attention or stand out. Practically, this means attracting traffic to your website—your main online marketing tool.

C is for Convert. Conversion happens when you turn a stranger into a consumer or customer. And there is a difference between the two! A consumer may take in your information or even sample your product, but he or she may not always buy. That's okay! Over time, that consumer may become a customer. The more expensive a purchase, the longer it may take. This means that you constantly have to work to convert people into consumers *and* customers.

T is for Transform. You transform when you turn past and present successes into magnetic forces of attraction.

Let's use Sue as an example. Sue sells quilts on the internet. So do hundreds of other people. How can Sue bring people to her

website? If she uses Facebook, she could create an alb
quilts. Jane, a Facebook friend of Sue's, looks at the p
instantly thinks of getting one for her granddaughter. Sue
that Sue has placed a link to her website right below the pictures,
so she clicks over to her site. Sue has successfully ATTRACTED
Jane to her website.

> With social media, you are the publisher! The sooner you realize you are a
> publisher, the more successful your business will be. Wouldn't it be great if
> people relied on you and your business to help them in their careers and personal
> lives? It's possible, but you have to start thinking differently about the way you
> market. Publishing valuable, relevant, and compelling information targeted to
> your customers and prospects is the answer. What's your expertise? How does
> that expertise relate to your customers' pain points? Then create the story and
> reach people where they are at—through email, ebooks, blogs, social media, and
> more. Then watch the magic happen: you become the authority for that niche.
> You are the expert, and you may never have to actively sell again!
>
> **Joe Pulizzi,**
> *co-author of* Get Content. Get Customers

Once Jane visits Sue's website, she takes a closer look at the
quilts. She finds one that she thinks her granddaughter would
just love but realizes that she can't afford it just yet. She makes
a note to herself that she will make sure to come back closer to
Christmas. Now, what are the chances that Jane will actually be
back? Very slim. Luckily, Sue has a newsletter sign-up box on
her home page. She offers Jane some tips on quilt making in
exchange for her email address. Jane gladly gives it; she is CON-
VERTED from a stranger to a consumer. Now, Sue can email Jane
whenever she has something exciting to share—a new shipment,
some more tips, or even news of a sale. Come Christmas, Jane
receives an email from Sue reminding her to get her Christmas
shopping done—and Jane buys. She is CONVERTED from a
consumer into a customer.

Jane loves the quilt she receives from Sue! It even has a nice note. Jane's granddaughter loves the quilt just as much. In fact, she drags it around the house. It has become her favorite blankie. Jane just has to take a picture and send it to Sue. Sue takes this picture and shares it on her company blog. She TRANSFORMS the success with a customer into an attraction tool. She explains how each quilt leads to long-lasting memories and how happy it makes her to see her customers happy. Enter Don. Don has been thinking about purchasing a quilt for his own daughter but wasn't sure if she would really enjoy it. He just stumbled across Sue's blog after his wife forwarded him an article in which Sue was featured. Seeing Jane's granddaughter's smiling image with the quilt makes Don smile. He thinks, "If that little girl loves it so much, perhaps mine will too." He also notes how much Sue seems to care about her customers. He buys a quilt instantly.

AHA! Zen Moment

In this book I'll be using the words "customer" and "client" interchangeably to refer to both, because there isn't much difference between them when it comes to using social media marketing techniques: you can ATTRACT, CONVERT, and TRANSFORM both with the same methods! 🧘

Through the ACT process, Sue ensures that she will never be short of customers. It is a simple yet effective process.

Start thinking about *all* your online marketing tactics as falling into *at least one* of these categories. Anytime you think about marketing, ask yourself this question: *am I using this technique to Attract, Convert, or Transform?* Keep in mind that there are plenty of instances in which an online marketing tactic can perform multiple functions. We will cover these instances later.

Attract

Nowhere is social media marketing *more* successful and useful than in the "attracting" phase of online marketing. During the attraction phase, you are trying to drive traffic to your site and stand out from the masses.

We will look at the exact *how* of driving traffic later in the book. For now, let's focus briefly on what you *need* in order to make your product or service attractive online.

This may seem like a detour from social media marketing, but it is in fact the framework you *absolutely* must have to attract people to your product or service.

What do you need to attract prospects online? A great BOD!

- **Brand**: If your brand could be summed up in one word, what would it be? I will use my company, The Marketing Zen Group, as an example. Our clients use many words to describe us, but at the end of the day, the best phrase is "one-stop shop." We constantly aim to provide anything our clients may need as it relates to marketing online.

- **Outcome**: What's the outcome you help clients achieve? Not the process you use but the *final* result. Sum it up in one line: *My company helps businesses grow by leveraging the internet.* Simple. We may create websites and conduct social media trainings and so on, but those are all part of the process. We do those things to accomplish a goal. That goal is to help our clients make more money. That goal is our outcome.

- **Differentiator**: What makes you *inherently* different from your competitors? For example, the online marketing field is a competitive one. However, most online marketers are *too* pushy for professional companies. The long sales pages, the scarcity tactics (buy now or forever hold your peace), and the like are just too much for many companies. This is where my company (The Marketing Zen Group) decided to stand out. We recognized that there is a need for solid online marketing for reputation-based professional companies. It has been an amazing differentiator for us! So, your differentiator, in other words, is simply what makes you stand out.

I can't stress enough how important these principles—these basic building blocks—are to online marketing and social media marketing in particular. There is no lack of information and noise out there. As consumers, we are constantly inundated with data. It is a continual Persian bazaar. If you don't have the right elements, you can't stand out from the noise. If you don't stand out, you can't attract people to do business.

The branding principle "everything communicates" has only been magnified by the rise of social media.

To be effective in this space, you have to be clear about what you want to be known for—what your brand stands for. And then, you have to be vigilant about building an integrated marketing presence that supports your identity consistently. Due in part to the blurring of personal and professional identities online, you can "leak" messages that are incongruent with your brand. Frustrated offenders might say, "I didn't want *that* to communicate!" But it's not our choice; the experience of the target audience determines our identity, and *they* decide what to include as an element of our brand.

From its essence to its look and feel, business model, affiliations, and so on, it has never been more important to thoroughly plan your brand.

Samantha Hartley,
Enlightened Marketing (www.EnlightenedMarketing.com)

The #1 reason people fail at social media marketing is that they don't have a solid foundation. They don't have a brand, they don't understand the outcome they provide, and they have absolutely no way of differentiating themselves from the competition.

Social media is the ultimate amplifier. If you have a good product or service, it will be amplified until it is perceived as great. If you have a shoddy product to begin with, that will also be amplified. Think about when you speak to your friends. Do you tell them that a restaurant you liked was *good*, or do you say it was *amazing*? Inside each of us is a storyteller. We like to amplify. Social platforms and the internet in general allow us to do that. They are a megaphone for your message. The people who consistently do well using social media are the ones who were already doing well to begin with. The medium simply amplifies their success.

Convert

So, what happens after you attract clients or customers? If they are an ideal fit, they convert. I say *if* they are an ideal fit because not everyone you attract will be. In our story earlier, Sue attracted Jane, who was an ideal fit. She was looking for quilts to buy. Let's say Sue also attracts Edgar to visit her site because he likes the pictures of the quilts on her Facebook profile. However, he doesn't have any use for a quilt; he just thinks they are pretty. He may never buy. And that's okay. You want to convert the Janes out there, not the Edgars.

As I mentioned previously, conversion can happen in one of two ways: (1) a stranger turns into a consumer, or (2) a stranger turns into a client or customer.

People become consumers when they subscribe to your blog, get on your newsletter list, or merely join your Facebook group (more on this later). They are *consuming* your information. At this point, they have converted. They are no longer strangers.

Why is this important? Even if they aren't paying for the content they're consuming, they are still being exposed to your company and your brand. There is an old marketing adage that says a person must come into contact with your brand seven times before he or she will make a purchase. Seven times!

Think about the last time you went grocery shopping at a big chain store. Chances are that there was some table setup that allowed you to sample a product—whether it was a new juice or old-fashioned jam. Studies show that when people sample, they are more likely to buy! This same "sample table" concept also works online. Offering people a sample of your work—whether through written content, pictures, or videos—can also lead them to buy from you.

Ideally, the formula works like this:

Consumption of Valuable Content + Time = Client

Time is a variable. Some people may buy right after sampling your product or service. Others may need much longer. Some of our clients received our newsletter for over a year before they decided to become clients. And not *everyone* should turn into a client. You only want those who are a perfect fit. The more qualified the buyer, the fewer the returns.

Consumers and business buyers want to make up their own minds about what they need without interference from noisy marketers. In fact, by the time they are ready to talk to you, they will be armed with information about your company, its people, and its products.

Benefit from this new buyer behavior by engaging with them as they search for answers. Deliver content that is relevant and compelling in their search for solutions. You can do this before they ever call you or walk through your front door.

You become the expert your future buyers can count on. Your content engenders a trusted relationship that makes it easy to buy from you. That's what content marketing is all about.

Newt Barrett,
co-author of Get Content. Get Customers

How Does Social Media Marketing Fit When It Comes to Conversion?

Let's be completely honest about what social media *rarely* does: lead to instant clients. For example, if you are looking to put up your LinkedIn profile and immediately get swamped by client requests, you may be disappointed. I won't say that social media marketing doesn't ever lead directly to clients because it does happen, but this should not be your goal. If you want to gain clients quickly, there are better ways of achieving it.

What social media is great at is turning strangers into *consumers*. It's the perfect channel for allowing people to get a taste of your product or service—it's sampling made easy.

AHA! Zen Moment

Social media marketing works best as a tool for attracting traffic and attention. It doesn't work as well for converting strangers into clients. It's better suited to converting strangers into consumers (i.e., blog readers or newsletter subscribers), if simply because "free" is an easy sell. Free works! And over time, it can and will lead to business. 🧘

What's the Best Conversion Tool?

Your website! There is *no* getting around this one. You shouldn't be engaging in social media marketing if you *don't* have a website first. Every time I speak on the subject of social media marketing, someone inevitably asks me, "Can't I substitute a social media profile (say, on Facebook or LinkedIn) in lieu of a website?" The answer is *always* no.

Why should you have your own website and not depend on social media profiles?

- **You *own* your website.** You don't own your social media profiles. Your profile (and your hard-earned contact list) is owned by the social media site itself. If it goes "poof" tomorrow, then so does your online presence.
- **Social media profiles are limiting.** You can convey only so much information on your profile. Although it may (and should) intrigue someone, it isn't enough to make a sale. Remember, social media is not a selling tool! It is an attracting tool.

Transform

Once you have mastered the art of attracting and converting, you must transform your successes into attraction magnets. This brings the entire online marketing process full circle.

People, especially strangers, crave social proof. Social proof is the theory that we are more likely to do something when we see others doing it. This applies even *more* when the others in question are similar to us. We often decide what to do (including whether to buy) based on what others are doing. This isn't the only factor in our decision making, but it is a major one.

Social media is built on social proof. Because of this, social media is a great way to transform past successes into new attention for your company.

There are two parts to transforming:

1. **You have to do a good job.** If your service or product just doesn't deliver, you are out of luck. You can't transform a bad experience into an attraction tool. Let's say you sell a blender and it breaks. The customer tries to return it, but your overworked employee says you just don't take returns. Sorry. And good day! This is not an experience you want amplified. On the other hand, if you do a great job, it makes for the perfect story. One of our clients is K9Cuisine.com. They sell premium dog food online. Nothing too glamorous, but their customer service is amazing. They go above and beyond just delivering an order. If a client orders regular shipping, they upgrade it for no extra charge. If a customer says his dog didn't like a specific brand, they swap it out and help him find something that his dog will like. They're more than just a dog food seller; they become trusted dog nutrition advisors who care about your four-legged friend.

2. **You have to *use* your success to attract more success.** This goes beyond just regular testimonials. This involves telling your customers' *story*—the story of what they achieved

through your service or product. When K9Cuisine.com receives an email thanking them for helping Jack, the loved golden retriever, start eating again after a long illness, they ask the customer if they can share their story with others. The story then makes its way onto their Facebook page and into their tweets. Soon, lots of people know about how K9Cuisine.com helped Jack. Next time they think about Fido needing dog food, they will think about K9Cuisine.com. If they have a great experience, they may tell their friends. The cycle continues.

Traditional marketers didn't worry about who controlled the message. Online marketers today engage an empowered customer. For this reason I ask my clients to keep two principles in mind at all times:

Make it easy to buy. This involves telling the right story, exposing the real benefits, and making your shopping cart a one-click affair. It helps keep you focused when you are creating your online presence and figuring out how you will construct your marketing message.

Pick tactics last. This ensures that you won't get distracted by the latest shiny-object fad before you have your essentials in place. Once you do, you can focus on picking the right tactics to really hear your customers.

Stephanie Diamond,
author of Web Marketing for Small Businesses

What Does Social Media Marketing Have to Do with This Step?

Everything! Whereas social media may not be ideal for converting strangers into clients, it's an excellent platform for sharing stories. Stories establish your expertise, attract fresh consumers, and even help convert faster.

The following are possible tools for transformation.

- Testimonials from customers and clients
- Case studies that showcase how a customer found a solution

to his or her problem (ideally the solution is your service or product)
- Video interviews with clients
- Audio interviews with customers
- Pictures of smiling clients with your products

AHA! Zen Moment

Social media platforms are a great way to showcase past and present success stories. By letting the customers speak for themselves, you can leverage social proof to attract more prospects.

Overview of Online Marketing Tactics and How They ACT (Attract, Convert, Transform)

The following table presents several online marketing methods and how well they accomplish each step of the ACT process. (Note: Search engine optimization (SEO) involves increasing the traffic to a website from search engines by causing the website to appear higher in a list of search results. SEO is discussed in more detail in Chapter 2.)

Method	Attract?	Convert? Consumer or Customer	Transform?
Social media marketing	Yes	Yes: consumer, not customer	Yes
Website/blog/podcast	Yes	Yes: consumer and customer	Yes
Email marketing	No	Yes: consumer and customer	Yes
Giveaway on site to build email list	Yes	Yes: consumer	No
Search engine optimization (SEO)	Yes	Yes: consumer and customer	No
Video	Yes	Yes: consumer and customer	Yes

One-Minute Online Marketing Secret

Have you ever heard of putting strategy before tactics? A strategy is an overall plan. It is the big picture: *what* needs to be accomplished and *why.* Tactics, in contrast, address the *when, where,* and *how.* Tactics are the way you implement your strategy.

Strategy should always come before tactics. However, most people doing business online go about this backwards. I call this the "shiny toy syndrome." They see the next cool networking site and join, or someone tells them they have to have a blog, so they start one only to abandon it after a month. I see people constantly chasing the next cool thing online without really knowing specifically what they want to accomplish. They may think, "I want to make money," but don't go further than that. And most importantly, because they don't know what they want to accomplish, they don't know how to measure the success of their tactics.

Are you trying to attract? Convert? Transform? Once you decide what your goal is, look at the table above to find a tactic that will help you achieve it. Then you'll also know how to measure your success. For example, if you *know* that the ad you are going to put on Google is meant to attract, then you will measure the number of visitors to your site to gauge how successful your investment was. You won't waste your time being frustrated that it didn't lead to more direct sales. If you were using a tactic to convert, you would check the number of people who subscribed to your newsletter. (Hint: These subscribers would be considered consumers! Remember: Consumption of Valuable Content + Time = Client.)

Now that you have a solid understanding of how social media fits into the bigger scheme of things, let's take a quick look at how to make the most of your ultimate conversion tool—your website!

Websites, Blogs, and SEO

YOUR WEBSITE IS A WINDOW into your company. If eyes are the window to a person's soul, a website is the window to a company's soul. Okay, okay, so now you know why I am sticking to writing nonfiction. My point is your website is crucial.

Social media, blogging, search engine optimization, and email marketing are powerful ways of developing online leads for most business. However, it's your company's website where your prospect makes a buying decision and the sale actually takes place. Each webpage needs to provide prospects with a compelling reason to do business with you, including calls to action that gently direct them down the sales funnel, getting them to "buy now" or contact you. While an unprofessional website will derail the best web marketing campaign, a well-designed site is a powerful conversion tool that will continually deliver high-quality leads.

Rich Brooks,
president of flyte new media (www.flyte.biz)

The following are three reasons you *must* have a website.

REASON 1: It's expected! Can you imagine a business that doesn't have a phone number? No telephone? How 1800s! No website? How 1990s!

As social media grows and companies break new ground, even a website may not be enough. What starts out as "all the cool companies are doing it" soon turns into standard practice. I wouldn't be surprised if future consumers get frustrated because they don't find the company they are trying to reach on Twitter. As communication channels increase, so does our level of expectation.

REASON 2: It's efficient. A website can multiply the number of people your business can influence exponentially.

Let's say you sell art supplies at a beautiful store. How many customers can you serve at one time? Two? Three? Maybe you are really good and you can serve four at a time. How many people can visit your website at once? Hundreds, thousands, maybe even hundreds of thousands. They can see your products, make purchases, and share you with friends—*simultaneously.*

One of the things I pride myself in is that we have made our virtual offices paperless. We don't have brochures or any printed marketing materials (aside from business cards). Our website contains everything a prospect might want to know about us. It includes case studies, articles, bios of team members, and even videos! And all of that is available 24/7, whenever our potential clients might need it.

REASON 3: It converts! Perhaps the biggest reason to have a website is that it takes care of the "C" in our ACT blueprint. A website can convert visitors that you attract (using social media) into consumers and customers. You can attract all the people you want on Facebook, Twitter, and LinkedIn. But if they don't convert, what's the point?

Why Your Website Can't Just Be Good—
It Has to Be Great!

Your website is the online equivalent of your office—the place people go when they want to do business with you. It's not enough to have just any website. People expect that your website will match their perception of your business.

Let's say you meet a guy at a party, and he is dressed to the nines. He tells you that he helps business owners triple their income. You also hear from someone else that he is a successful business consultant. You chat with him for a few minutes, and you are impressed! This guy looks like the epitome of success. Then, he pulls out a business card (also fancy) and invites you to his office. You think, "My business could always use more help. It couldn't hurt to visit with this guy." So you go to his office.

Except his office is hard to find. You drive around for thirty minutes in circles before you locate the building, and when you finally find it, it's more like a broken-down warehouse. You park your car, double-check the locks, and slowly make your way in. The office is decrepit. It is a congested little room with papers strewn all around, and to top it off, it smells like cat litter.

Will you still do business with the guy? You might. But you may also see a major disconnect in his public persona and his actual business. If your website isn't up to par—easily findable and professional—this is the same disconnect people are likely to feel about you.

Our web is not the web of the 1990s. Remember when people actually "surfed the internet"? It was common and many times it was listed as a hobby. "I like to read, take long walks on the beach, and surf the internet." Surfing is over. It was easy back then because there were fewer websites. Today, there are trillions of websites, and people have a lot less patience for bad ones. Think about it: how long do you look at a website you are unsure about before you hit the back button? According to Canadian researchers, web users form first impressions of webpages in as little as fifty milliseconds (1/20th of a second). In the blink of an eye, we decide if we will keep looking or go back. This is why good enough isn't good enough anymore. You have to have a great website.

Website 911–EMS

To be great, your website must do three things simultaneously. It must Educate, Market, and Sell (EMS). Whenever I hear that someone's website isn't doing what it needs to, I always find it lacking in one of these three areas. And EMS is essential when it comes to conversion.

Imagine that all the visitors to your website are dots on a scale from 1 to 10. At 10, a visitor becomes a client or customer—the ultimate goal. Now, imagine a whole bunch of dots scattered on that scale. Some are at 1, some are at 5, and some are at 9.

The ones at 1 are just being introduced to your brand. They just heard about you and have landed on your website for the first time. They need to be educated about how you work before they will buy. (Note: The bigger a sale, the longer the education process may need to be. You don't think too hard before spending $20 on a book, but you may need more time when you're buying a $20,000 car.)

The people at 5 already know you. They may even trust you. They just need to be nurtured for a while longer. They may need more education, or they may need more marketing—or they may just be waiting for the right time. If you are there when the time is right, the 5s are likely to buy. Let's say you sell Halloween costumes. I may not buy until Halloween comes around, unless another event comes along for which I need a costume. But when I do feel the need, it's important that you are already positioned as a solution.

The 9s may be ready to buy but just need the right incentive. Perhaps a final reminder? A last question answered? A discount? Whatever it is, your website needs to provide it to make the sale.

My goal here is to show you that everyone who visits your website will be at a different point on that imaginary scale. Your website—through Educating, Marketing, and Selling—has to move all the visitors who are an ideal fit to 10.

Let's take a look at which elements allow a website to serve as the ultimate marketing tool.

Five Elements of a Great Website

A great website has impeccable design, structure, content, optimization, and maintenance.

DESIGN: Looks matter. So much so that scientists have a term for the way looks affect us: the halo effect. The halo effect occurs when we think something looks good on the surface and so we broaden the scope of that positive judgment to include characteristics other than outward appearance. If someone is good looking, we infer that he or she must also have a good disposition. The same concept applies to websites. If a website looks good, we assume that the company behind it must also do good work. First impressions count. Especially online, where a visitor doesn't have much to go by except your website.

STRUCTURE: Ever visited a website and were confused about where you should go? Too many choices boggle the mind. And when our mind is boggled, it is easier to say no than yes. The way you structure your website navigation is crucial. The structure must guide visitors through your website and hand-hold them (virtually) into taking action. And it must do this for visitors at every level—those who may be ready to buy now and those who are first-time visitors.

CONTENT: Content is king. It is the heart of every good website and serves multiple purposes. The first purpose is to educate prospects and build expertise. This is why blogs are so heralded. A well-written blog can help you stand out from the competition and educate your prospects. (I talk more about blogs later in the chapter.)

You can provide content in several forms: written (blogs and articles), audio (podcasts), and visual (video). Want to really kick it up a notch? Provide content in all three forms. This is not overkill; it's about appealing to the various learning preferences of a potential visitor. In this day and age, choices rule. Give your visitors a choice, and they are much more likely to choose you.

Content becomes especially important if you are in the professional services industry or any business-to-business field in which expertise plays a key role. Content is also the lifeblood of search engines. Think about it: search engines are looking to serve their customers with good search results. They constantly have to separate the wheat from the chaff. They have to differentiate spam sites (websites set up specifically for the purpose of spamming people—think Viagra emails) from real, wholesome websites (like yours!). One of the ways they do this is by looking for content. The more fresh content you provide search engines like Google to deliver to their customers, the more the search engines reward you.

OPTIMIZATION: Optimization has two meanings here. One, your website has to be optimized internally. A website may look beautiful from the outside, but if the inside is poorly built, chances are it will start to show. For example, if it isn't coded correctly, it can look odd in certain browsers even though it looks fine in others. The World Wide Web Consortium has a tool that allows you to make sure your website is well coded. The tool can be found at jigsaw.w3.org/css-validator. You just put in your website address, and it will tell you what, if anything, needs repair. The second type of optimization relates to search engines and making sure that search engines can "read" your website. This is called search engine optimization, and it is discussed in detail later in the chapter.

MAINTENANCE: The website of today in many ways is a living, breathing thing. In the past, you could create a website and sit back. Today, you can't. Passively keeping a website is almost akin to opening a store, stocking the shelves, and then doing nothing. You don't have to re-create the store every day or even every year, but you do need to tag products, move items around, change displays, and so on. Your website is the same way. Once you have the design and structure in place, you don't have to keep changing it. However, you do need to maintain it by adding content.

AHA! Zen Moment

Blogging can be a great attracting *and* converting tool! People can find your posts attractive and subscribe to your blog, becoming instant consumers. Over time, they can be converted into customers.

A blog is an instantly and easily updatable website. A blog is the hub of your social media strategy, enabling you to grow your online presence as social media trends change and evolve.

Andy Wibbels,
author of BlogWild! A Guide for Small Business Blogging

Blogging

All blogs are websites—they exist on the web, and are reached using a web address—but not all websites are blogs. Blogs have these elements in common:

- Content is regularly updated. Search engines love this!
- Content is generally broken down into "posts" (akin to articles).
- Posts are presented in a reverse chronological order (newest first).

- Readers can leave comments. This is excellent for interacting and building a fan base.
- Content is syndicated (published in multiple places at the same time) via an RSS (Really Simple Syndication) feed, allowing people to subscribe to your blog. Every blog has its own unique RSS feed. Anyone can subscribe to your blog's RSS feed and read it using a "feed reader" or a "feed aggregator." There are lots of different feed readers out there. My favorite is Google Reader, which can be found at www.google.com/reader.

AHA! Zen Moment

RSS feeds can allow you to distribute the same content to more than one location. You can have wide visibility and gain exposure by distributing the same content strategically to multiple social networks. ⚖

The Million-Dollar Question: Do I Need a Blog?

You don't need a blog, but you do need fresh content on an ongoing basis. The best place to put this content is in a blog. Can you choose to just post this information on a webpage? Yes, but it isn't nearly as efficient because readers can't subscribe, and you can't keep up with your consumers to turn them into clients.

Blogsites

You can add a blog to an existing website, but you can also build a website around a blog. I am a huge fan of hybrid websites, or blogsites, where the entire website is built on a blogging platform. There are many blog publishing platforms out there, but the one I use is WordPress. It is the most robust platform, and many business websites are now using it as a content management system (CMS). A CMS allows you to manage your entire website like you would a blog. You get an admin console from which

I started my blog four years ago and always had it separate from my business website. Right before my book launched this year, I decided to move to an integrated "blogsite" platform on WordPress for the following reasons:

- **Effort and resources.** It was taking too much time to update both a blog and website with relevant information. And without changing information on the website, why would people come back after an initial visit? By having an integrated site, people come back over and over to read new content.
- **SEO.** I realized that I was not being efficient by driving people to two sites. It became confusing to know which link to provide when sharing my bio, and I was diluting the SEO for both sites. Now every road leads to one site, which has increased traffic and Google ranking.
- **Client conversion.** I had many people visit my blog who loved my posts but who did not have a complete picture of what I did professionally. Many did not click the link in my "About" section to my main website to find out about my products and services. Since converting to one site, I have had a twofold increase in individual coaching clients, as well as strong sales in my live workshops and membership site.

Pamela Slim,
Author of Escape from Cubicle Nation

you can edit your site, allowing you to maintain your website and make regular changes without much technical knowledge. If you don't have a technical background or a webmaster who can make your updates, you should consider getting a content management system.

Search Engine Optimization (SEO)

My good buddy and colleague, Steve West, from Profits on the Web is one of the smartest guys I know when it comes to SEO. Not only that, he explains it in such a neat way that I asked him to walk us through the optimization process using a fictional site.

WordPress is the ultimate publishing platform because it's easy to use, it's not overly complicated, and it's infinitely flexible. Sure, it's great for blogs, and that is its forte, but it's also great for non-blog websites and even ecommerce sites. Because of plug-ins and themes (especially Headway, which includes visual blog design tools), WordPress can be extended into anything you can imagine. Creating and publishing content in WordPress really is about as easy as writing an email, only instead of clicking "Send," you click "Publish." That's such a satisfying button to click on, too, because whenever you do it, you know that hundreds or even thousands of people are going to read what you wrote.

Michael Martine,
Remarkablogger (remarkablogger.com)

Search engines pose one of the biggest challenges to website owners and webmasters. Optimizing your website so that it is logged by search engines in a way that's most beneficial to you is much more than adding a few keywords in a meta tag. Search engines do not actually see or read webpages. They see individual characters (letters, numbers, etc.) and character combinations (words, phrases, etc.). When a search is performed, the search engine compares a query (the search phrase) to various segments of a webpage, including textual content, image alt tags, meta tags, and other factors. Proper search engine optimization, or SEO, presents a webpage to the search engine with emphasis on specific combinations of characters.

Because webpages number in the billions, it takes a lot of work and a solid strategy to get your home page near the top of its relevant search results. Please make note that *relevancy* in all things, above all else, wins the search engine ranking game: the more relevant a search engine thinks the content of your website is to a visitor's search, the closer to the top of the results that search engine will place your site.

With that in mind, let us begin the process. We'll use a website for a fictional dentist as an example.

Step 1: Target Your Intended Market.

What does this have to do with SEO? Everything!

Write a description of the kind of person you would most like to visit your site.

> **EXAMPLE:** Parents with school-age children. The families should practice proper dental hygiene and believe regular dental maintenance and checkups are important. They should live in middle- to upper-class neighborhoods with a household income in the $70,000 to $150,000 range.

This brief description will help define how your website should communicate to your visitor. It should be obvious from the dentist's site that the clientele he wishes to attract can afford, and is willing to pay for, regular dental care. This might seem self-evident and unrelated to SEO. However, it is amazing how many times a dentist looking for this type of client will rank well in specialized dentistry searches like "orthodontists" or "oral surgeons" yet cannot be found by families searching for "family dentists."

A search for "family dentistry" found 10.2 million webpages. A search for "family dentists" found 16.1 million webpages. Significantly, the top ten sites were different in these two searches. The average internet user will consider these searches to be the same and will also find that the websites they receive contain very similar content. However, the search engine clearly "saw" huge differences in the two searches, because it returned different results.

With this knowledge, and a description of the desired site visitor, we are ready for the next step.

Step 2: Target Your Search Phrases.

This step seems simple but can be very difficult. It requires thinking like the site visitor you targeted in step 1. You may need to forget your technical knowledge during this step. For instance, our dentist feels "prophylaxis" is an important phrase for his business. However, even if his future patient knows the technical term for preventative health measures (such as teeth cleaning), she may not know how to spell it.

Develop a list of words or phrases for which your target visitor is most likely to search. Keep the list short. It is easier to drive traffic with half a dozen carefully considered words and phrases than hundreds of them.

The list of words and phrases you develop in this step will provide the information necessary to create relevancy in the steps that follow.

Step 3: Write and Edit Page Content.

The principle behind this next step is so obvious and self-evident that most people, including site developers and SEO specialists, ignore it: *content is king.*

This bears repeating. *Content is king.*

By "content" I am referring to everything on the page that your website's visitor sees.

"Wait a minute," you say. "You just said that *relevancy* wins the ranking game." That's still true. Content is king; relevancy is the power behind the throne.

If the typical target visitor does not speak "geek," then don't use geek speak. As a general rule, when writing your content, use the language your target visitor will use when searching. The exception to this rule is when you are educating the site visitor. But remember, your website can only educate a visitor who has found it to begin with.

Incorporate the most important words in your content. Your high school English teacher might disagree, but repetition in your content is a powerful tool for search engine optimization. As long as your content reads logically, you will run little risk of getting blocked by search engines for overusing a word (overusing a word or phrase without regard to logic can lead search engines to think you're a spammer). This section, step 3, is a prime example of optimized content. It has been written to attract search phrases that include the word "content." The word "content" appears 19 times in 302 words.

In addition to the obvious text content on a page, every graphic *not set as background* is another opportunity to communicate relevant content to a search engine. Although a search engine cannot see images, it does read their alt tags as content. The alt tags attached to buttons, logos, diagrams, charts, eye candy, and the like all represent content that search engines can read. Images are an excellent way to subtly repeat content you want to emphasize.

Once your content is written, it is time to target the search engines.

Oh, yeah, don't forget: *Content is king!*

Step 4: Tag Your Website.

There are four basic tags to make sure you create for every page on your website.

<title>Your Title Goes Here</title>

The page title tag does not carry a lot of weight with most major search engines but it does reinforce other content elements. This tag is considered the official title of the page and appears at the top of your browser window, above the address bar. Write the title to reflect the most important search words or phrase represented on that page. Use a different title on every page with relevant content. Some pages, such as a "Contact Us" form, may not contain any real relevancy for search engines. Tag them anyway, but use your company name or domain name as the title instead. Use title case in this tag.

<meta name="title" content="Your Page Title Goes Here" />

This tag is what actually tells the search engines what the title of your website is. Typically this is identical to the title entered in the previous <title> tag. Although both of these first two tags are called "title tags," they serve different purposes. Always include them both. Use title case in this tag.

<meta name="description" content="Describe what this page is about in this area." />

Use this tag to tell the search engines what your webpage is about. Your description should include the search word or phrase most commonly used in the content. If possible, use the word or variations of it two or three times in the description. Many, but not all, search engines display the content of this tag in their search results, but do not make the mistake of writing the description to sell the internet user on the value of your product or service. The goal here is getting your site to the top of the search engine result lists. Use sentence case in this tag.

<meta name="keywords" content="your keywords, your key phrases, and dominant relevant words go here, separated by commas" />

Use this tag to tell the search engines the keywords and phrases that are relevant to your site. There is no magic to keywords. Keywords are not the magic bullet that will drive your site to the top of search results. That said, keywords can provide very powerful augmentation to your website's content. When properly developed, they help establish the all-important relevancy: they tell the search engines whether the content in the website is relevant to the search phrase being queried. If you have used target words effectively in your content, the keywords and phrases to use in this meta tag are easy to figure out. Use the words and phrases you came up with in step 2, and make sure to separate them with commas.

In the case of our dentist, let's say his targeted words and phrases are "dentists" and "teeth cleaning." His tags might look like this:

```
<title>ABC Family Dentists Teeth Cleaning and General Den-
    tistry in Arlington</title>
<meta name="title" content="ABC Family Dentists Teeth Clean-
    ing and General Dentistry in Arlington" />
<meta name="description" content="ABC Family Dentists gen-
    eral dentistry and teeth cleaning in Arlington provides den-
    tistry services to families." />
<meta name="keywords" content="dentist, dentistry, teeth
    cleaning, general dentistry, arlington dentists, general den-
    tistry in arlington, teeth cleaning in arlington" />
```

Although these tags represent poor writing skills if you're trying to communicate to a human reader, keep in mind they are written for search engines, not people.

If you follow the steps in order—

1. Target your intended market
2. Target your search phrases
3. Write and edit page content
4. Tag your website

—you will find the process relatively simple. It is a lot of work, but then, you are competing against thousands if not millions of webpages.

And always remember: *content is king; relevancy is the power behind the throne.*

> "Social media marketing is the process of promoting your site or business through social media channels, and it is a powerful strategy that will get you links, attention, and massive amounts of traffic."
>
> Maki,
> *Dosh Dosh*

Social Media Marketing: What You Need to Know Before You Start

The Nature of the Fun-Loving Beast

Now that you have a solid understanding of online marketing, we can move on to social media marketing. Let's break down the phrase "social media marketing."

- **Marketing**: Promoting a product or a service to increase sales
- **Social media**: Online platforms where people connect and communicate

Some examples of online platforms are blogs; social networking sites such as Facebook, Twitter, and LinkedIn; and YouTube.

Most people abuse social media platforms. They use them to push their message on people and try to dominate the market. Remember our discussion about the mistake of going against the grain? This is a great example. Marketers who abuse social media usually do so because they are used to using traditional marketing methods like television. You can't talk back to the TV. (Well, you can, but it doesn't get you very far.) With social media, talking back is the whole point; it's a conversation, not a monologue.

Chapter 1 discusses how traditional marketing has evolved over the years. Now let's take a look at a table of descriptive words and phrases that compares traditional marketing and online marketing—specifically, social media marketing.

Traditional Marketing	Online Marketing/Social Media Marketing
Dominate the market	Create a community within the market
Shout out loud	Listen, and then whisper
Me, me, me	Us, us, us
Push the product or service	Pull in people with your message/story
Advertising	Word of mouth
Control	Allow
Pursue "leads"	Nurture relationships

Why Social Media Marketing? Why Bother?

According to a recent Razorfish Consumer Experience Report, 49 percent of web users have made a purchase based on recommendations they received through a social media site. Yet only 25 percent of businesses have a Facebook page, and many fewer use any other social media platforms. Marketers are missing out on a huge opportunity to connect with potential customers. Social media marketing is a good idea for the following three reasons.

1. **Social media sites are where the *people* are.** Let's say there was an expo happening with *250 million attendees,* and I offered you a free booth. Would you take it? I sure hope you would. That's how many people are using Facebook. If Facebook was a country, it would be the world's fourth largest, smaller than the United States but larger than Indonesia. And it costs nothing to join.

2. **Trust in advertising continues to erode.** Let's face it. We trust our friends more than we trust what the nice folks on TV tell us. You can either *be* that friend or you can be the voice on TV that gets ignored. The call is yours. But you can't fake it. Because of the transparent nature of social media, you can't really hide who you are for long. Let's say a company pretends that they value their customers more than anything. Then they turn around and treat a customer badly. That customer has a voice. Chances are she has a Facebook profile or Twitter account. Even if she doesn't, she may tell a friend who does.

3. **People are already talking about you.** That last example tells us something else, too: people are already talking about your products, your service, and your company. It's inevitable. Social communities are breeding grounds for interaction. The only choice you have is whether you join the conversation.

Two of the most powerful benefits of social media for small business are access and prominence. Tap your blog to demonstrate thought leadership (aka prominence) in your niche, and then leverage Twitter and Facebook to expand the conversation, facilitate evangelism, and grow your "following." As an example, Twitter lets you find highly relevant conversations with prospective clients, vendors, mentors, and colleagues in real time; join in, demonstrate value, and then, if appropriate, offer solutions to any problems being discussed. Do this on a regular basis and you'll grow a sizable tribe primed for your products and services.

Jonathan Fields,
author of Career Renegade

Social Media Marketing Tenets

Before we delve into the nitty-gritty of specific social media platforms and how to make the most of them, let's look at the tenets of social media marketing. These principles do not change, regardless of the technology in question.

- **Respect other people online.** Whether you're using email or instant messaging (IM) or social media: (1) don't spam people, (2) don't blindly add people to your email list, and (3) respect people's "virtual space." Basically, follow the Golden Rule; if it would annoy you, it will doubly annoy another. The same common rules of etiquette that apply offline apply online, too. Would you ever run up to someone, hand him your business card, and run away? I hope not. Yet people often do the online equivalent: post their website link—their virtual business card—blindly on people's online spaces.
- **Efforts to control or manipulate will backfire.** Did you hear the story of how the CEO of a top grocery chain got busted for pretending to be a customer and praising the company in forums? It was quite a scandal. Once his identity was

made public, it was all over. It's next to impossible to manipulate people online without getting caught. And because there are *so many* better ways to go about influencing people positively, there is no need to control the conversation.

- **Don't chase everything new under the sun.** This is a common mistake many people make when first starting out. Remember "shiny toy syndrome"? Resist the temptation to grab at everything. Do your research, pick one or two methods, and work at them consistently. This is the reason I am not covering in this book every social media channel that's out there. I've chosen instead to focus on the ones that I believe provide the highest return on investment.

- **Traffic is nice but should not be the only goal of social media marketing.** Some people out there look at social media marketing *only* as a means of attracting traffic to their websites. Although traffic is a great goal and easily measurable (it falls under Attract), it should not be your only goal. Remember, you can and should use social media to transform as well. It is a great way to share your stories, listen to feedback, and cultivate relationships with potential customers and future partners and vendors.

- **It's a good idea to use your *real* name.** Nine out of ten times, it's best to use your real name—even if you represent a company. Why? People don't want to be friends with McDonald's or Dell. They want to connect with others like them. We cover later when it is advisable to use your business name.

- **You have to be proactive.** This is not the same as being pushy. I hear the following a lot: "I am on Facebook and LinkedIn, but it doesn't seem to do much." My response is usually, "What exactly did you expect 'it' to do?" It's like saying you went to a networking event that didn't do anything for you. The real question here is what did *you* do at the networking event? Did you reach out to two people and have a conversation? Social media is only what you make of it.

Social Media Marketing Checklist

The following is a list of what you *must* have in place (or be in the process of putting in place) before you start with social media marketing. Remember: social media marketing is only part of the bigger picture.

- ✓ **A good BOD**: You must have a keen understanding of your brand, outcome, and differentiator.
- ✓ **A website**: Remember EMS. Your website must educate, market, and sell!
- ✓ **Content**: Ideally, your website will include a blog, because a blog makes it easy to update your site regularly with fresh content, but however you update, just make sure you do. Fresh content increases the likelihood visitors will stick around and turn into consumers.
- ✓ **An email capture mechanism**: Don't send people to your website unless you have a way to follow up with them. Ideally, this means collecting their email addresses so you can send them relevant content in the form of a newsletter or bulletin in the future.

Have all four? You're ready to rock and roll!

Visibility + Credibility = Real Social Media Success

By using social media to position yourself as an expert in your field, you'll stand out from competitors, generate buzz, and increase your value. To do this, you must market yourself as a highly visible, ideally matched source of information for your audience.

Always focus on providing valuable content, boosting your credibility, and building trust. When done correctly, you'll turn followers into loyal fans who practically do your marketing for you.

Value, credibility, and trust. Add those three things to a high level of visibility and you have the social media recipe for success.

Nancy Marmolejo,
Viva Visibility (www.VivaVisibilityBlog.com)

Which Technologies and Networks Do I Use?

Although there are thousands of social networking sites and technologies out there, in this book, I will be focusing here only on the three that I have found to be the best for marketing purposes:

- Facebook (www.facebook.com)
- Twitter (www.twitter.com)
- LinkedIn (www.linkedin.com)

I also cover certain technologies that complement social media marketing, including online video.

There's really only one way "social" and "marketing" can coexist happily. And that's if you take off your marketing hat when thinking about social media marketing and, instead, think like an average user of social media.

Allow yourself to become engrossed in the user experience on social media sites. Watch for things like how the particular "culture" of each site is constructed and maintained. Watch for things people say and do that would lead nicely into relationship building, which leads to new clients, branding, or product sales.

Since it is impossible to completely forget that you are a marketer, you will still pick up on great ways to increase business through social media, but you must think like a user first and a marketer second.

Social media users are there for anything but advertisements and pushy marketing. But make no mistake about the fact that marketing is being done successfully on these sites. It's called social marketing for a reason, and it's a very different thing that you can only see when you have your user goggles on.

Once you understand the main purpose of any social site, you can do a lot to increase your traffic and grow your business with social media in ways that don't turn off users, but that engage, intrigue, and excite them.

Jack Humphrey,
FridayTrafficReport.com

For each of the three networking sites, I'll tell you:

1. Why to bother with it
2. How to use it
3. Do's and don'ts
4. Specific marketing tactics

Ready? Let's get started!

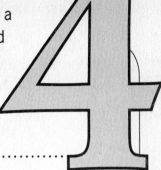

Facebook

With 300 Million Users and Growing, This Giant Can't Be Ignored

Why Bother with Facebook?

- Facebook has more than 300 million *active* users, and it's growing every day.
- More than half log on at least once a day.
- More than half are out of college.
- Its fastest-growing demographic is those twenty-five years old and older.
- It offers fantastic online visibility for your brand.

Facebook is like a coffee shop. Everyone is there for his or her own reasons, but it is a great place to strike up a conversation.

People from all walks of life use Facebook. They aren't there to buy stuff. They are there, first and foremost, to express themselves. After self-expression comes their need to connect with others.

Research shows that people use Facebook primarily to showcase their own identity—not just who they are, but who they want to be perceived as. The friends we make, the groups we join, and the pages we fan on Facebook are all offshoots of this basic identity creation and re-creation.

This is why you can never push products or services on Facebook. If you try to convert people directly to customers or clients, you will fail. However, if you are looking to attract consumers and build relationships over time, you will succeed. Your goal on Facebook should always be to attract people to your website, build trust, and gain visibility—all things that inevitably lead to sales.

AHA! Zen Moment

Think about how you can be a part of people's identity. Remember the cool kid everyone wanted to be friends with in school? Why did everyone want to be that person's friend? Because it meant he or she was cool, too! You want to position your brand so people want to make it part of their identity. 🧘

How to Use Facebook

Facebook can be divided into four main parts: profiles, groups, pages, and events. Each part serves a certain function, and each has to be used uniquely.

Profiles are a way for people to present themselves. Each person gets his or her own unique profile. You cannot share a profile, and you cannot create a profile for a business or any other entity.

Groups allow people to create subcommunities within Facebook around a topic of interest. There are serious groups such as "Small Business Owners" and silly ones like "I know what you did last summer."

Pages, or fan pages, are for essentially anything and anyone that someone would care to fan. Everything from Oreos to rock bands can have a page.

Facebook events can be set up to attract participants to any live or virtual event.

Facebook recently changed its look, and the look of many of its components has also changed. This is often referred to as the "new Facebook." Facebook has gone from being a just a social network for college students to a social center for people and businesses from all walks of life, and it has had to evolve to keep up. But although Facebook is constantly changing to keep up with demand, a lot of the basics remain the same.

Your Facebook Profile

This is where it all begins. Your Facebook profile is your personal space, your billboard, your calling card! A profile is *not* for businesses. A Facebook profile is for individuals only. Your profile is created automatically when you sign up for a Facebook account. If you don't want to connect your personal name with your business, find an employee who is willing, because you can't do anything—join groups, manage pages, and so on—on Facebook without first having an account.

Your profile is how you ATTRACT people initially, as well as how you get them intrigued enough to visit your website (off of Facebook). You attract them by showcasing your expertise and sharing value.

To make sure you understand how to make the *most* of your Facebook profile, I use my own profile as an example.

Left Column

Let's look at your left column first.

Your picture is the first thing a person notices on your profile. Avoid goofy or inappropriate pictures (unless that is part of your brand). I highly recommend investing in a professional headshot. This will come in handy across the social media sphere. Avoid any type of group picture or party picture. Your profile pictures should showcase you, and you alone, in the best possible professional light.

View Photos of Me (183)

View Videos of Me (16)

Edit My Profile

This area is a glimpse at your photo albums. Pictures are a great way to humanize a face behind a company or product. They say, "Hey, I am just like you!" That being said, avoid inappropriate pictures. You can wreck your reputation, and even lose your account over it.

I have hit the 5k limit on FB Friends. Please join my page – http://www.facebook.com/sh amakabani

– President of The Marketing Zen Group
– Social Media Specialist
– Speaker/Trainer
http://MarketingZen.com
http://Shama.Tv

Since the "new Facebook" emerged, this section has become extremely important. The old Facebook showcased your entire profile, including the information now under your Info tab (see p. 45), when a friend clicked on your name. Now, your "Wall" is what shows up first, so what you write in this box may be the only information someone sees about you. This box is ideal for a quick synopsis and web link. Don't be vague. Use it to establish your brand—who you are!

The information box is another area that gives a really good synopsis of you. A network, simply put, is any place you belong(ed) to and wish to stay connected to. Be sure to search for your college, as well as the state you live in.

This box shows a random selection of six of your friends. If you are viewing someone else's profile, Facebook will also show you how many mutual friends you have. This is key because it gives you a good way to grow your network on Facebook—you can ask a mutual friend for an introduction if you don't feel comfortable introducing yourself to someone directly.

This area gives a quick overview of your pictures and videos. As a speaker, I post my speaking videos in the videos section. If you are an artist, you may want to post pictures of your art. If someone else tags a picture of you that you do not like, you should feel free to un-tag that picture. Your profile is your personal space, and you can choose what is and is not appropriate.

Facebook Notes is an application that comes with your profile and is a great way to share important content with your friends as well as an opportunity to brand yourself and communicate your expertise. If you have a blog, you can import your entries as notes. Every time you post a new entry, Facebook will automatically create a note of it. Go to "My Notes" and click "Import a Blog." The application walks you through the rest. You can also create your own notes specifically for Facebook by going to this application and clicking "Create a New Note."

Right Column

The right column is much wider and is your creative space!

This header shows the different areas within your profile. If the person looking at your profile isn't your friend, he or she can't see your Wall unless you have made your entire profile public. Once a person becomes your friend, the first thing he or she sees is your Wall—a place where friends can leave you notes and where you can start discussions via status updates (see below). The Info section contains your full profile—i.e., your hobbies, favorite movies, etc. It includes whatever you have chosen to share. In the Boxes section, you can showcase other applications you may have added.

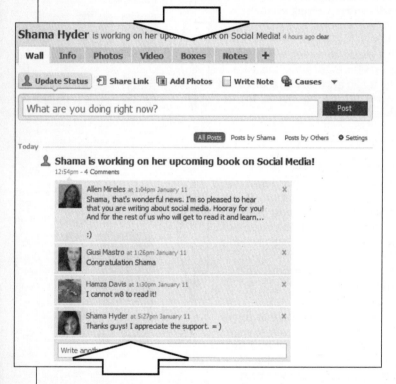

Facebook allows you to share what's on your mind via status updates, which show up on your Wall and on the news feeds of your friends. You can use your status updates to start and engage in conversation. You can ask questions, share links, and update your friends about your business. You can also attach photos and videos.

Status Updates (Your Wall)

When you log in to Facebook, you are asked: "What's on your mind?" This is a very tricky question, because—let's face it—lots of thoughts run through our minds, and if we shared all of them, it would create a lot of noise. No one really cares if you just had breakfast, are getting an oil change, or just dropped off your kids at school.

Use the status updates in a strategic way. Share important business news; announce events, give advice, and provide *value*. Status updates are really the heart of Facebook, because they create an ongoing impression of the person posting them. "Oh, Joe—he is such a partier. Just look at his Facebook updates!" "Jane—she is such a giver! She is constantly sharing tips with us." Only share when what you are doing matches your brand and provides value. In the following example, I mention that I am finishing up my book. This reminds people that I am writing a book; it builds curiosity! Plus, it's good information for anyone awaiting its release to have.

 Shama is putting the finishing touches on her book! a moment ago - cle

What are you doing right now?

Status updates are also great for starting conversations. You (and your friends) have the ability to comment on any status you post. It's a quick way to build to stronger relationships.

Shama Woo-Hoo! Client now ranks on the 1st page of Google for "Dallas IT Outsourcing." All within 1 WEEK of launching site!!! =). via Ping.fm - 1:24pm - Comment

Shelle Michaels at 1:26pm December 11	X
!!!	

Maria Reyes McDavis at 1:26pm December 11	X
Congratulations you talented Diva!	

David Aubin at 1:32pm December 11	X
That's awesome! I've been trying to get higher SEO for awhile now. Excellent job! :)	

Michelle Church at 1:45pm December 11	X
WOW - I am impressed - excellent - sooo when will you start teaching us how!!Congratulations	

Bob Sommers at 1:56pm December 11	X
Congratulations!	

Trey Scalf at 2:14pm December 11	X
Kudos!! I will benefit greatly from your hard work!!	

Eugenie Verney at 2:18pm December 11	X
Wow! That's impressive!	

Alison Eliason at 3:11pm December 11	X
Congratulations! You deserve it!	

The following are three stories that illustrate how I have leveraged Facebook Notes and status updates to further my business.

1. **Snagged a speaking engagement**: I posted that I was speaking at a local Dallas–Fort Worth event on Facebook marketing. Another local, Elizabeth Marshall, caught the update and asked if I was willing to speak to her group on the same topic. I said yes, and we soon discovered that we were alums of the same high school—and even shared a favorite teacher! Liz and I have gone on to become good friends and have partnered on many occasions since.

2. **Received a press opportunity**: One day I got a phone call from a local TV station. They were doing a segment on Facebook and wanted to interview me. How did they know about me? A reporter from Austin had seen my updates on Facebook and knew I spoke on the topic. She'd given them my name.

3. **Established expertise**: Search engine optimization (SEO) is a part of what my company does. When we succeeded in getting one of our client's keywords in the Google top ten, I posted an update about it. It was a great way to showcase our work because it established our expertise in the area and reminded people of what we can do. It also showcased my genuine excitement over our results.

Information Section

The information section is where you want to showcase yourself in the best light. Whereas everything else on Facebook gets updated fairly regularly, this area remains more or less the same—unless you change your favorite movies on a regular basis!

Fill out your information section as professionally and purposefully as possible. I can't stress this enough. Even though this is your personal profile, people will judge you professionally by it. This doesn't mean you can't have a life. By all means, share your interests and hobbies—but don't share anything that you wouldn't share with a stranger on the street.

Your profile information should be entered with a purpose in mind. Are you going to use Facebook to attract more people to your business, or are you going to use it to attract your next job? What do you want someone to walk away with after looking at your profile?

Did you know that lawyers can look up your Facebook profile and use it to *judge* whether you should be on a jury? Yes, the information you put up on Facebook can be used as evidence in a court of law.

Your information section is broken down into a few segments:

- The first segment is your basic information.
- The second segment is for "personal information."
- The final segment is where you can share your education and work history.

Basic Information

Networks:	Texas Alum
Sex:	Female
Birthday:	April 25
Hometown:	Dallas, TX
Relationship Status:	Married to Arshil Kabani
Interested In:	Men
Looking For:	Networking
Political Views:	Moderate
Religious Views:	Faith is the cornerstone of all religions

The first segment is your basic information. This is what people will see first. Keep it honest and professional.

Personal Information

Activities:	Working on my business, helping clients understand and leverage the internet to increase revenues, reading books and blogs. Constantly implementing new ideas and taking rapid action. I am an editor at heart. Create, Edit, Re-Create is a Motto.
Interests:	Entrepreneurship, Reading, Writing, Blogging (Business Blogging), Video Blogging, Small Business, Personal Development, Baking Chocolate Moltens, Antiques, History, Vintage, Shopping, Technology and Business, Communication, Speaking, Training and Development, PR, Marketing, Publicity, Online Marketing, Social Media Marketing, SEO, Learning New Things, Teaching, Networking.
Favorite Music:	Does NPR count? =) Eclectic. Bollywood, Pakistani Pop (Atif Aslam), Country (Leann Rimes, Taylor Swift, Brad Paisley to name a few...), Dido, Jewel, Sarah Mclachlan.
Favorite TV Shows:	Frasier, Journeyman, Charmed, Lisa Williams, King of Queens, Rome, Rachel Ray, Rome, True Blood, John Edwards, Aliens in America, Legend of the Seeker, Absolutely anything on the the History Channel!
Favorite Movies:	Too many to list, but I usually love the historical fiction pieces. All Time Favs: Amazing Grace, Grease, Rounders
Favorite Books:	When you read a book a day-this becomes a very complicated question. :)
Favorite Quotations:	To laugh often and love much; To win respect of intelligent people; And the affection of children; To earn the approbation of honest critics And endure the betrayal of false friends; To appreciate beauty; To find the best in others; To give one's self; To leave the world a little better, Whether by a healthy child, A garden patch, Or redeemed social condition; To have played and laughed with enthusiasm And sung with exultation; To know even one life has breathed easier Because you have lived... This is to have succeeded.

The second segment is for "personal information." This is a great area with which to build rapport with someone. The information you give here is what I call "coffee talk." If you were going to go have coffee with a potential client or vendor, what are some of the things you'd share? What would you want them to know? You can share those things here.

Education and Work

Grad School:	Texas '06 M.A. in Organizational Communication, Communication Studies
College:	Texas Communication Studies
High School:	R. L. Turner High School
Employer:	The Marketing Zen Group
Position:	President
Time Period:	February 2006 – Present
Location:	Dallas, TX
Description:	I started my first business when I was 9 years old. It was a gift wrap selling business, and I used to spend hours flipping through the catalog and feeling the silky samples. I could tell azure blue from shocking red with my eyes closed. The business was a flop, but I learned three important lessons.

1. Never hire your six year old sister as your assistant–even if she works for candy.
2. Don't make sales calls using the Yellow Pages.
3. Your parents will only buy so much gift wrap before their customer satisfaction level drops.

The lessons didn't exactly stop there. I went on to start and build 3 successful businesses, but nothing was greater than the thrill of marketing them online. What most people hated or didn't understand (marketing), I loved. Go figure.

Since launching The Marketing Zen Group (formerly known as Click To Client), I have helped dozens of companies leverage the internet to attract more clients and increase profits.

These days you can find me on the national speaking circuit (...speaking about online marketing and social media marketing), on Twitter, and on Facebook. And of course, working with our FABULOUS clients from my office in Dallas, Texas.

In my free time, I enjoy working (no, really, I am addicted to my work!), spending time with my family (this includes my puppy, Snoopy, a.k.a. the office mascot), reading (I read a book a day–no, I am not joking), and watching movies.

The final segment is where you can share your education and work history. Use the work description area to tell a story about what you do and how you got there. Allow people to connect with you through your story. If you are looking for a job, write about what your ideal career would be.

Facebook Vanity URLS

Not too long ago, Facebook began allowing people to choose a vanity URL that would easily allow them to share their profile address. Instead of having to search for friends or memorize a long Facebook URL (usually filled with random numbers and letters), you could create your personalized URL to direct folks to. Mine, for example, is www.facebook.com/ShamaTV. You can create yours by downloading Facebook's "Memorable Web Address" application (more about applications later in the chapter). Be sure to get one that matches your name and/or brand. Since my web TV show is called Shama.TV, and just Shama was taken, I went with ShamaTV. You want to avoid anything vulgar or random, such as StarWarsLover or CutiePie123. First try your first and last name or a combination thereof. Don't be disheartened if the name of your choice is taken; Facebook vanity URLs are not the be-all and end-all of your social networking experience.

Facebook Privacy Settings

In recent months, Facebook has created some very robust privacy settings, allowing you to decide who gets to view what part of your Facebook presence. For example, you may allow everyone to see your basic profile but only a select few to see your pictures. You can control your privacy settings by choosing Settings and then Privacy Settings from the top menu bar.

A word of caution here: although you can certainly make things private, nothing is 100 percent secure. Facebook, after all, is just a website. It can experience glitches. If a glitch occurs and your private information is made public, make sure it isn't anything that would cause you embarrassment. Also keep in mind that your Facebook friends may share your information with others—intentionally or unintentionally. I personally know many people who let others, such as bosses or spouses, use their account to browse Facebook.

Again, never share anything—publicly or privately—that you wouldn't be comfortable sharing with a complete stranger.

How to Build Your Facebook Friendship Base

Does the number of friends you have matter? Yes, to a degree. Does this mean you should obsess over building your numbers? No. Having more friends is great, because it means you have a bigger pool to network with. You can use Facebook to keep up with current customers and vendors, and you can also use it to meet new people. But a lot of people get stuck on the word "friends" and equate their friend number with their worth. Remember that on Facebook, "friend" just means someone you know.

You do want to focus on having a high-quality group to network with. Let's look at three ways you can start building a quality friendship base.

1. **Use the tools that Facebook provides when you first create an account.** One tool will look through your email address book to see who in it is already using Facebook. This is a quick way to find people you already know. You can send a friend request to anyone you want, but start with good friends and colleagues so you can start to build your network fast. Also, don't be surprised if the first time you log on, you see friend requests waiting for you to approve. More people than you realize may already be on Facebook and looking for you!

2. **Bring offline networking online.** When you go to conferences or mixers and bring home a stack of business cards, search for those people on Facebook, and add them as friends. Then throw away their cards! Facebook will even remind you of their birthdays.

3. **Use a forwarded domain name.** Facebook allows each profile a vanity URL but, to make it even easier for your friends to find you, buy a domain name and have it forwarded to your Facebook profile. Mine, for example, is www.ShamaHyder.com. That URL takes you directly to my Facebook profile. You can also create unique domain names for your Facebook groups and pages. This technique is especially useful if your name is more common.

Marketing with social media has created an equal, level playing field for this new era in business. It has given personal brands an opportunity to compete with big brands. Entrepreneurs don't have to have a big budget or a lot of capital to position themselves as a thought leader in their industry. As someone who started without a big following, database, or big budget, marketing with social media gave me the chance to position myself as an authority in the marketing arena. Now anyone with a passion and a message can do the same thing and build a loyal tribe.

Alejandro Reyes,
Successfool.com

Creating a "Friending" Policy

The most common dilemma people encounter on Facebook is who to "friend." When "friendship" is loosely defined as a network of associated contacts, how do you proceed? The best way to go about this is to have a policy in place before you start using Facebook. Some people only accept people as friends after having met them offline. Others have an open-door policy. You have to choose what you are comfortable with. However, if you are using Facebook to market your business and attract new people, then you don't want to close off your network to only those you know. My policy is open door: "friend" unless proven otherwise. I reach more people through my work and my speaking engagements than I know. To keep the doors of communication open, I welcome all I meet to connect with me on Facebook. If someone spams me or does something inappropriate, I remove him or her. (On the bottom left of each person's profile is a "Remove from Friends" link. That's all it takes.) I discuss how to create a social media policy for your overall business later in the book.

Facebook Groups

Facebook groups are a great way to meet (and collect!) people with similar interests or problems (that you can solve!). A Facebook group can be formed around any topic or idea, and you can directly message up to 5,000 members. The best part is that you can message all the members in your group, and the message goes directly into their inboxes as if you had messaged each of them individually. Groups are very much like online forums. Forums are a modern equivalent of a traditional bulletin board: a place where users generate content, host discussions, and create a community of sorts. On Facebook, the owner of a group serves as its moderator.

Whenever one of my clients is considering a forum, I recommend that he or she look into Facebook groups first. They are a fabulous way to create your community for free. You can find groups by clicking on the Groups icon (on the left side of the bottom menu bar). From the Groups page, you can use the Browse Groups link to search for ones that match your interests, or you can use the Search field to search for specific groups. You can also invite friends to join your group. A person doesn't have to be your Facebook friend to join your group, but you can (and should) invite friends you think would be interested to join. You don't want to invite people blindly, however. Let's say your group is all about stay-at-home moms. You want to specifically invite those friends who you know are moms.

If you want to create a community and provide value, I highly recommend starting your own group (which you can also do from the Groups page). ACT Blueprint is my Facebook group for people interested in online marketing (see the graphic on p. 56). I use it to provide value, attract more people to my brand, and educate at the same time.

Remember: You cannot message all the members in your group once you have more than 5,000 members. However, don't worry about this when you are getting started. Chances are that Facebook will increase these limits over time.

Do not create a group around your brand or business. This is what (as we will soon discuss) pages are for. Groups are best built around an idea, a thought, or a topic. Online marketing is a topic that I am very passionate about and, hence, I have built a group around that.

Think about the problem your company solves. Then build a group around that topic. What if there is already a group with that topic? Great! Get involved in it, but follow the rules. If you see a group you like, you can simply click "Join this Group" on the right-hand side of the group's page. Some administrators allow everyone to post; others moderate. You can also find a different angle on the same topic and start your own group. There isn't anything wrong with this. You are entitled to build your own community.

What all can you do with Facebook groups?

- Mass-message group members (up to 5,000). Facebook members tend to have a higher response rate than email lists. This is great for converting members into clients or customers over time. When this book first came out in ebook form, the majority of buyers were members of my ACT group.
- Provide value and increase visibility. This way, more people see you and recognize you as an expert.
- Post relevant pictures and videos. This provides content as well as helps your group members feel like they are part

of the community. Let's say you run a wedding dress boutique, and you start a group called "Brides-to-Be Unite!" where you provide tips on how to have a great wedding. You can post pictures of your latest dresses and create short videos on how to choose the right dress, how long should you wait before you go shopping for it, and how to fix last-minute tears.

- Use the discussion board to start meaningful discussions and discover problems that your potential clients or customers may be having.
- Build a community of people who trust you. Kevin Kelly, cofounder of *Wired* magazine, posted on his site an excellent article called "1,000 True Fans." It argues that you don't need millions of fans to do well. You just need 1,000 people who will buy everything you sell and trust you to serve them. He was talking about bands, but the concept applies to everyone. If you are a consultant, for example, you don't need 100 companies to hire you. You need maybe ten or twenty that will consistently hire you to produce results.

The following are six ways you can promote your Facebook group.

1. Make it easy for people to join your group! Buy a domain name for your Facebook group and have it forwarded to the Facebook group address (which is always long and difficult to remember). For example, www.ActBlueprint.com will take you directly to my Facebook group. You can put the domain name on your business cards.
2. Share the link to your Facebook group on your profile. Include a note about why you created the group and what you hope members will get out of it.
3. Put the URL for your Facebook group in your email signature.
4. Invite friends from other social networks to join.

5. Invite your website visitors to join by placing a graphic button on your site.
6. Host giveaways and contests for your current members so word gets around.

———— AHA! Zen Moment ————

You don't have to manage your group(s) yourself. You can assign multiple administrators for each group. Ask your assistant to join as an administrator, and let him or her invite new members to the group, post articles, and alert you if there is a question specifically for you. Outsourcing group upkeep, while still staying connected to the people in the group, is a great time saver. 🧘

Facebook Pages

Facebook pages, or fan pages, as they are sometimes called, were created in late 2007 because Facebook wanted to give businesses a space for their brands but didn't want businesses to create profiles, which Facebook reserves for people. If Facebook finds that a business has created a profile instead of a page, they will close the account. This is why you should keep your profiles personal and create a *page* for your business.

Pages are much more customizable than groups, and you can have an unlimited number of fans. The best part is that pages are indexed by Google. By default, all fan pages are public. That means if someone searches for your company or for keywords that you cover in your page, your page will show up in Google's search results. This is an easy step toward search engine optimization. However, you cannot mass-message fans the same way you can your group members. Fan page updates show up in people's status updates (on their Walls) but not in their inboxes. This used to matter a lot, because updates were hard to locate on people's home pages, where they rarely clicked. Now updates are listed directly below messages in user inboxes.

Should You Create a Fan Page or a Group?

Both are important for different reasons, but start with a fan page. If you are an established company, like K9Cuisine.com (whose page is shown below), then you should absolutely focus on your page first. You will notice that the fan page looks a lot like the profile and has many similar attributes. A page also allows you status updates, an information section, a tab for more applications, and more.

A group is a great way to build a closed community that you nurture over time, whereas a fan page is a public platform for reaching more people, and it provides more visibility for your brand. It is also great for building a community but sacrifices a "small group" feel for public visibility.

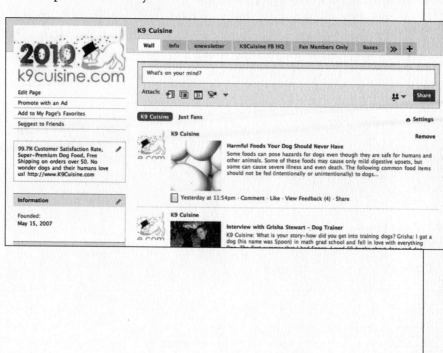

How to Promote Your Facebook Page

You can promote your Facebook page the same way you would a Facebook group: by sharing the link on your profile and adding it to your email signature, letting your website visitors know about it, and inviting other people to become fans.

You can also purchase a domain name for your Facebook fan page, but once you hit 1,000 fans, Facebook will allow you to have a vanity URL for your page. You can use this URL instead of the longer URL that you're initially given.

Facebook Events

Facebook's events feature allows you to promote any event or milestone. It doesn't even have to be a physical event. Virtual events, like teleseminars and webinars, also qualify.

When you create a Facebook event, you get a full page featuring your event (which looks much like a group or page). An example of an events page is shown below.

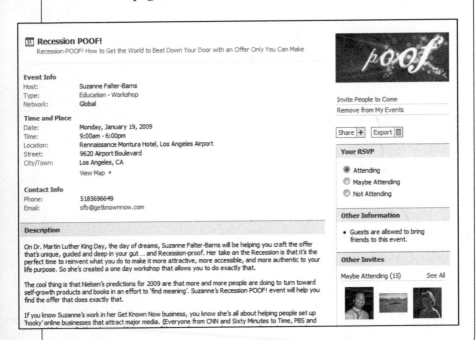

You can invite friends to your event, ask them to invite their friends, and even collect RSVPs.

As it does with pages, Facebook allows indexing of public events. This means SEO benefits for you!

What kinds of events can you promote?

- Local live events
- Live events in other cities
- Performances
- Book signings
- Teleseminars
- Virtual events
- Product launches
- New store openings
- Nonprofit events (walks, benefits, etc.)
- Parties
- Educational classes
- Meetings (formal or informal)

How to Create an Event on Facebook

Click on Applications (found in the left corner of the bottom menu bar), and choose Events from the pop-up list. Then click "Create an Event" (located at the top right on the applications page). You will be given a simple three-part form, like the one below, to fill out. Note that you can host an event personally or host through a group you moderate.

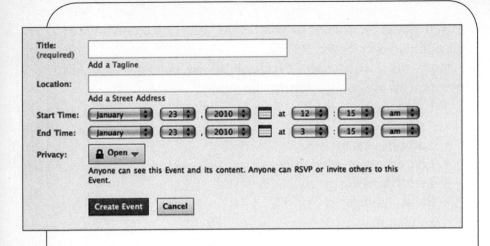

Title:
(required)

Add a Tagline

Location:

Add a Street Address

Start Time: January | 23 | , 2010 | at 12 | : 15 | am

End Time: January | 23 | , 2010 | at 3 | : 15 | am

Privacy: 🔒 Open ▾

Anyone can see this Event and its content. Anyone can RSVP or invite others to this Event.

Create Event | Cancel

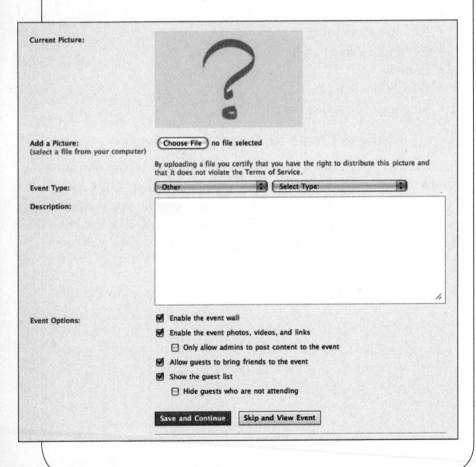

Current Picture:

Add a Picture:
(select a file from your computer)

Choose File no file selected

By uploading a file you certify that you have the right to distribute this picture and that it does not violate the Terms of Service.

Event Type: Other | Select Type:

Description:

Event Options:
☑ Enable the event wall
☑ Enable the event photos, videos, and links
  ☐ Only allow admins to post content to the event
☑ Allow guests to bring friends to the event
☑ Show the guest list
  ☐ Hide guests who are not attending

Save and Continue | **Skip and View Event**

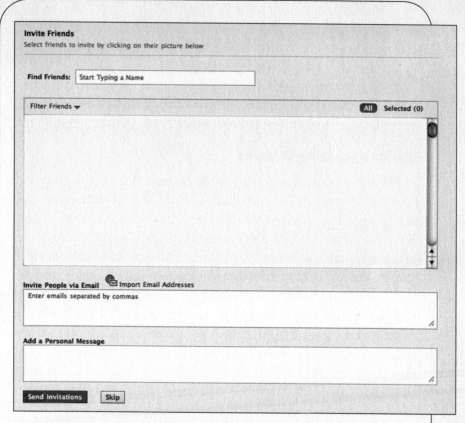

Keys to Promoting Your Event on Facebook

Follow these six guidelines:

1. **Choose a catchy title.** I get at least five event requests a day. I only look at the ones that catch my eye.
2. **Create a clear and thorough description.** It's annoying to see one-liners. "Join Us" isn't a description. Show people what's in it for them.
3. **Include time zones.** Facebook has users on every continent—including Antarctica. Remember to select the appropriate time zones in the description area.
4. **Invite your guests to bring their friends.** You want to get the word out, right? Encourage your friends to invite other friends. But...

5. **Don't invite blindly.** Spend some time thinking about who might benefit by attending. Add this to your description: "You are being invited because...."
6. **Post pictures and video.** Did you host the same event last year? Share those pictures! Give people something that will help them get a feel for the event.

About Facebook Applications

Applications, also known as widgets, are the reason you get snowballs "thrown" at you and virtual gifts. Applications are also what allow you to take quizzes like "Which *Friends* Character Are You?" In the old Facebook design, applications were easily noticeable on people's profiles. The new Facebook doesn't emphasize applications. Most applications aren't developed by Facebook but by outside companies.

Can you use applications as a marketing tool? I don't usually recommend creating applications as a marketing tool for small- to medium-sized businesses unless the applications have a very specific tie-in to the product. For example, a company is creating a Facebook game. To promote their game, they may introduce an

Marketers need to be where their customers and potential customers are and, increasingly, this is on social networking sites. Social networks are emerging as a powerful and sophisticated new kind of marketing channel. Marketing is becoming precise, personal, and social; social networking sites are giving marketers new abilities to hyper-target campaigns using profile information, engage community members by tapping into social capital within friend groups, and systematically cultivate word-of-mouth marketing across their existing customer base. For many products and services, recommendations and referrals from trusted friends and colleagues are important factors in deciding whether to buy.

From The Facebook Era: Tapping Online Social Networks to Build Better Products, Reach New Audiences, and Sell More Stuff *by Clara Shih (@clarashih on Twitter), who developed the first business application on Facebook and is currently CEO of Hearsay Labs*

application that goes with the game. For most companies, there are better (and more cost-effective) ways to market on Facebook. That being said, if you do choose to create an application, make sure you give users a chance to showcase their identity. Quizzes and other applications that allow an individual to showcase himself or herself work well. One popular application on Facebook is LivingSocial. It allows people to share five favorites in a number of categories—five things they wouldn't leave home without, five books they love, their top five restaurants, and so on. If you create an application, think about how you can cater it to the individual rather than making it all about your company or product.

What about adding applications on your profile? The new design really de-emphasizes applications, so I don't recommend adding many for marketing reasons. Also, feel free to ignore application requests sent by your friends. This isn't poor etiquette, and it will keep your profile from looking cluttered. Applications developed by Facebook itself, such as Notes and Videos, come with your Facebook account, and you should use them. A directory of applications can be found at www.facebook.com/apps.

About Facebook Ads

Because Facebook is teeming with people, it would seem to make sense that Facebook ads should be a great investment; however, Facebook ads still have a long way to go. People on Facebook aren't in shopping mode yet. They aren't even searching for information (as they might be while searching Google). They are looking to connect with their friends, update their profiles, and just stay current. What this means is that they are happy playing in the Facebook sandbox; they don't want to go outside Facebook to another site. However, ads can be used successfully to market Facebook groups and pages. Even if people don't click on the ads, you still get increased visibility when they appear.

The following information (provided by Jonathan Lyons) about an ad posted by the Peabody Memphis, a historic hotel in Memphis, Tennessee, is an excellent case study on Facebook ads.

The Peabody Memphis found tremendous success in advertising with Facebook ads for their annual rooftop party concert series. The rooftop parties are local concert parties lasting from April to July atop the hotel. Their goal was to increase cover revenue and beverage revenue by advertising a Facebook group. This group was geared toward a target demographic: males and females, ages twenty-one to forty, who live in or near Memphis and like to party.

Ad Name: The Peabody Memphis Events and Rooftop Party
Targeted group: 21–40 year-olds who live in Memphis, TN, and
    within 25 miles of Memphis, TN

The Facebook group served as the primary source of information about the rooftop party concert series. The hotel posted event announcements, prices, drink specials, band information, pictures, and videos. Members of the group also posted their own photos and videos.

Their advertising budget was $1,000. The ad had two lifetimes: the first from April 2, 2009, to April 14, 2009, and the second from May 4, 2009, to May 23, 2009. In total, it made more than 4 million impressions—meaning it appeared on its targeted group's Facebook pages 4 million times—and 3,796 clicks. Their average cost per click was $0.30. Before the ad ran in April, the group had 1,000 members. After the ad ran, the group doubled to 2,000 members.

As a result of the boost in exposure, the rooftop parties saw a significant increase in attendance, cover revenue, and beverage revenue from 2008 to 2009. Average attendance increased 113 percent from 8,487 to 18,018. Average cover revenue increased 162 percent from $23,205 to $60,702, and average beverage revenue increased 83 percent from $81,195 to $209,351.

The following are tips the hotel shared with me for advertising using Facebook ads.

- **Identify your goal.** What do you specifically want to do? For us, it was increase cover revenue and beverage revenue to a series of rooftop parties lasting from April to July 2009.
- **Be specific in targeting.** We targeted locations relevant to our business. Since the parties occurred in Memphis, we targeted that city. We also targeted adults twenty-one to forty, since it was a twenty-one-and-up party.
- **Use keyword targeting.** You can take targeting a step further by allowing your ad to appear only to people whose profiles use certain keywords. For example, next time we may target our ad to people whose profiles mention words or phrases such as "beer," "partying," "going out," and "downtown Memphis."
- **Make the ad clear, concise, and simple.** Ours read:

PEABODY ROOFTOP PARTIES
[picture of our rooftop party logo]
Join us for the 2009 Peabody Rooftop Party Season. Every Thursday, April 9–July 23, 6–10 P.M. $5 cover. Ladies get in free until 8 p.m.

- **Use a call to action.** Encourage the viewer to click the advertisement. For us it was "Join us for the 2009 Peabody Rooftop Party Season."

About Facebook Connect

Facebook Connect is Facebook's latest brainchild. It allows users to "connect" their Facebook identity, friends, and settings to any website. If you have ever commented on a blog, you probably had to provide your name, email address, and website URL. Now, if a website has Facebook Connect in place, you can simply log in to the website using your Facebook ID. As a website owner, you definitely want to have Facebook Connect set up on your website. It takes some technical savvy, but you can find all the directions at developers.facebook.com/connect.php. Now, not

If there is one thing I can emphasize that every brand should know about Facebook marketing, it's how to automatically share your customers' activities with their Facebook friends using Facebook Connect. Facebook Connect enables brands to integrate Facebook on their own websites, leveraging each user's already-built social graph of close friends and family to further promote and share what you are selling. Being able to leverage the Facebook social graph of each user enables you to increase page views, keep users on your site longer, and in the end convert those page views into sales! Learn Facebook Connect.

Jesse Stay,
CEO of SocialToo (SocialToo.com)

only can visitors to your website log in using their Facebook ID, you can see exactly who is visiting your website. And when they comment on your blog, it shows on their profile for all their friends to see as well. Your online visibility is amplified.

Facebook Do's and Don'ts

DO:
- ✓ Spend time creating an outstanding profile.
- ✓ Let your personality shine through.
- ✓ Reach out to people in a professional and thoughtful manner.
- ✓ Build a loyal Facebook friendship base.
- ✓ Leverage Notes and status updates by providing value.
- ✓ Work on attracting people to your site (using real value, not pushy links).
- ✓ Have a friending policy in place.
- ✓ Build a community around your topic or specialty.
- ✓ Be proactive in your networking efforts.
- ✓ Share relevant pictures and videos.
- ✓ Participate actively in groups.

DON'T:

- ☒ Be pushy.
- ☒ Post your web link when writing something on someone's Wall (it's blatant self-promotion and will usually be deleted).
- ☒ Send or accept frivolous applications.
- ☒ Use your business name as your profile name.
- ☒ Put up crude or thoughtless pictures or comments.
- ☒ Expect social media to "work" for you (you have to work it!).
- ☒ Be impatient (real relationships take time to build).
- ☒ Friend blindly (always let people know *why* you are requesting a connection).

AHA! Zen Moment

How should you ACT on Facebook?

Attract: Make your website address prominent on your profile. Write notes or articles about your industry. Leverage status updates to attract more people to your website.

Convert: You may not gain clients directly from Facebook, but you can gain consumers. Use notes and status updates to establish your expertise and give potential clients and customers samples of your work.

Transform: Post videos and use status updates to tell stories and share your triumphs with friends. Facebook is a powerful platform to showcase your current successes. Use it! 🧘

How to Be Proactive on Facebook

The following are actions you should take *daily* on Facebook.

- Approve any friend requests that you may have waiting for you.
- Wish friends a happy birthday. Facebook lists birthdays of the people in your network on the right-hand side. It takes five

minutes to wish twenty people a happy birthday, but it could make someone's day.

- Update your status with something meaningful and valuable. Reading a great article online? Share the link in your update.
- Quickly glance at your home feed and see if any useful updates catch your eye. Comment on them appropriately.

Take the following actions *weekly*.

- Reply to any relevant messages in your inbox. If you receive a group email and wish to reply to only the sender, click "Reply" and not "Reply All," which bombards the entire group.
- Drop in to the groups you belong to, and see if anything has been posted that strikes you as useful. There are some powerful groups out there, and really making the most of them can help your business dramatically. I run my ACT Blueprint group very much like a mastermind service—a *free* mastermind service. You can ask questions and get real answers to online marketing questions.
- If you have a group, invite new friends to join. Answer questions in the discussion forum, and post any relevant videos or articles.
- Post a note or a video. The idea is to go beyond an update that's just a few words long. Share something meaty.
- Pick two people in your network with whom you want to set up a one-on-one meeting. You can do this using Skype or instant messaging, or you can set up a phone conversation.
- Take the following actions *monthly*.
- Track how many people visited your website from Facebook, and measure which articles or posted links got the most feedback. Then do more of what works!
- Choose one person in your network who serves the same audience as you (but doesn't compete directly), and approach him or her about a joint venture. A joint venture

happens when two or more people team up for mutual benefit. Let's say you are a chiropractor. You might approach a massage therapist and see if you can refer business to each other. Or you might just offer to share some useful articles on wellness for his or her clients. Make sure you do your homework beforehand and have something of value to share. Don't worry if that person doesn't reply. Hone your

Facebook fan pages were created to be the official presence on Facebook for companies, nonprofits, and celebrities. Fan pages provide an incredibly rich opportunity for small and large businesses to interact with customers and fans, and find new customers and fans. You can think of fan pages as microsites—centered around a Wall tab, pages can add more tabs to feature Facebook applications such as Photos, Videos, Events, Reviews, and Notes, and even applications customized just for your company.

However, the major advantage of Facebook fan pages over microsites or your own company websites is that they are built on the Facebook platform—where a lot of people are spending a lot of time each day. To be precise, as of September 2009, 300 million users are on Facebook, with 1 million new users per day! Furthermore, Facebook ads allow you to "hypertarget" based on demographic information and keyword information found in profiles—not only to find out how many people in your particular target audience are on Facebook, but to reach them and draw them to your fan page. For example, an Italian restaurant in Cleveland can choose to advertise only to men and women ages twenty-five to forty who list "Italian food" as an interest. A Dallas florist can choose to advertise only to women within a twenty-five-mile radius of Dallas who list themselves as "engaged." Once people become "fans" of your page, you can interact with them on a regular basis, just as you would interact with your friends.

No matter what your business or organization, chances are now that your customers and potential customers are using Facebook. Why not bring your business to them?

Dave Kerpen,
Chief Buzz Officer of theKbuzz (www.theKbuzz.com)

offer and approach the next person. Joint ventures can be very powerful, but they must be done correctly. You have to be able to make a valuable contribution, and your audience has to be interested.

- Post videos or pictures from any speaking engagements you have done. If your company held an event or an office picnic, that's perfect as well. I find that pictures of a cute office mascot (a puppy named Snoopy, in my case) also work very well.

- Scan your current network and choose three people to message, and ask if there is anything related to your business that you can do for them. Be sincere, and follow through on your promises. This is how relationships (and leads!) are nurtured.

A Cautionary Note

I would be remiss if I didn't add the following warning. As you build your community on Facebook, be sure to drive it outward—to your website, your email list, and so on. Why? Because as much as you feel that you own your information and contacts on a social media site, you don't. If Facebook ever decides to ban your account (and I have seen it done, even to people who always followed the rules), you don't want to be stranded.

There is a new service, SocialSafe (www.SocialSafe.net), which for $2.99 will back up your profile, pictures, and a list of your friends. This is a very worthwhile investment. But even if you have this backup in place, I reiterate: use Facebook as a tool to attract, but constantly look to pull people to your site.

Twitter

The Fastest Growing Social Media Site

Why Bother with Twitter?

- It has 20 million users and is growing.
- It's the fastest-growing social networking site.
- Its largest demographic is thirty-five- to forty-four-year-olds.
- It provides excellent online visibility.
- It's a great way to attract traffic.
- It allows for instant communication.

Twitter is like a giant, colorful bazaar.

With only the 140 characters per tweet that Twitter allows, you can attract attention and create an expert platform like never before. Unlike with Facebook, you *can* get clients and customers directly. People use Twitter not just to connect with each other, but to share what they need, so it's *much* easier to spot people who might need your help on Twitter than it is on Facebook.

Twitter Basics

Let's start with some basic Twitter knowledge.

You get 140 characters to answer: "What are you doing?" This is the entire premise of Twitter. However, the worst thing you can do is *actually* answer that question. (I will get to that in a bit!)

Messages that people send out are called "tweets." "Tweeting" is another common phrase; it means sending a message via Twitter. Your tweets make up a timeline. When people subscribe to your timeline, your tweets show up on their Twitter home page. These people are called followers. You can follow them back if you choose. Unlike Facebook, following does not have to be mutual. You can follow anyone you want, but they don't have to follow you back.

Everyone gets a Twitter name. Choose one that's short and memorable. You can thank me for this later when your followers are able to retweet your messages more easily.

You don't have to reply to all tweets. If you want to reply to someone's tweets or want to get someone's attention, type @username and then your message. For example, let's say you want to tweet me. Currently I have over 17,000 followers, and only 10 messages or so show up on my home page. If you want to get on my radar, you can tweet: "@Shama—Thanks so much for the Twitter tip!"

Your home page will show a random assortment (chronologically) of messages tweeted by the people you are following. The image below shows my home page. When someone sends you an "@" reply, it will show up on your home page and will also be filed under your replies tab (the line under "Home" that reads @Shama, below). Replies are public, and everyone can see them.

You can also send direct messages to people. The 140-character limit still applies, and you can send only direct messages to people who are following you. This isn't the same as sending replies, which can be sent to anyone using the @ sign. Direct messages are hidden from public view and shown only to the recipient. To send someone a message directly, click the Direct Messages link in the

It's All About the Dialog!

While most of my friends consider me an early adopter, everything I get involved with already has at least a sprinkling of users, so I think I'm somewhere closer to the middle. Nonetheless, in the case of Twitter, I've had an account since it was a weird, unknown service with a funny name, long before Oprah and Ashton Kutcher created the race for followers and wayyy long before TV shows decided that a Twitter crawl on the bottom of the screen offered pretensions of interactivity.

Heck, in the old days, having more than 500 followers was an amazing feat, and those people who got into the four-digit follower numbers were the wizened elite, the really popular folk on the service. Now there are so many (spammy) tools to garner followers (none of whom are actually paying any attention to you) that it's common to see newbies who have thousands of followers and no clue how Twitter works.

Twitter certainly can be a one-way communication channel, a 140-character megaphone to an audience of thousands, but to do that is to miss out on what differentiates Twitter from the many other social media services available: it's interactive and lets you instantly *establish a dialog* with your customers and community.

I know Shama gets this, but I worry that you, the reader, might not. Please, to really understand the value of Twitter and to really gain benefit from your involvement, keep in mind that you need to *give more than you expect to receive*. Don't ask, "How many followers can I blast my message to?" but instead, "How many people can I engage in a dialog with?"

You'll be surprised just how much more enjoyable—and valuable—the experience will be.

Dave Taylor,
DaveTaylorOnline.com

right-hand column. This will open a window that allows you to type in the recipient's name and your message.

You don't have to use your browser to get on Twitter. You can use a desktop application. My favorite is TweetDeck (www.Tweet-Deck.com). There are also tons of mobile applications for Twitter.

Just search the internet for "Twitter application + [device of your choice]" (e.g., Mac, iPhone, etc.).

Many Twitter users use hashtags, words that include the hash symbol (#), to keep relevant tweets organized. Hashtags were developed by the Twitter community to make it easier to search for relevant tweets. They are very popular at conferences and seminars, where many people might be twittering, because they make it easy to track what is going on at an event. For example, during the Iranian elections, a lot of twitterers were updating Twitter with news. They would use the hashtag #iran or #irannews, so if someone was searching for tweets on this topic, he or she could find them easily. You can see current hashtags at hashtags.org and WhattheTrend.com.

Retweeting (RT) is reposting another person's tweet. This can have a quick viral effect when the quality of the information is good. For example, let's say you post a link from your blog. If I am following you and I like the link, I will retweet it to my followers. There are two widely used formats for retweeting:

- Type "RT @username" and then copy and paste their message.
- Copy and paste their message followed by "(via @username)."

Your Personal Twitter Page

Your Twitter experience starts with your Twitter page, or personal profile. This is different from your profile on Facebook, because it gives you less room to play with. You have to be succinct on Twitter. The following are some tips on how to make the most of your Twitter profile.

- Start by picking a short username. Ideally, go with your first name. Although Twitter allows you to use business names as handles, I recommend you go with your personal name. People want to be friends with people. If you are a big company looking to further your brand and provide customer service on Twitter, use your company name. If you have multiple employees using Twitter, you can create a co-handle—a handle that incorporates both the individual's name and the company's. For example, Mike-Nike and SteveCEO-Nike are co-handles.

- Use a good headshot. You don't get much space for a picture, so make sure it is large and clear and captures attention.
- The same applies to your bio. You get 160 characters for it, so be concise and direct. This isn't the place to be vague or wordy. Focus on what you do and/or who you help. Mine says: "President of ClickToClient.com, Web TV Show Host, Social Media Speaker/Trainer." I could also say: "Helping businesses leverage the internet as president of ClickToClient.com."
- You get one web address. If you have multiple websites or multiple businesses, pick one to showcase here. I choose to showcase Shama.TV because it allows people to get to know me as a person better, and because I point out my business URL in my bio.
- Get and use a personalized Twitter background. This is akin to your computer's desktop background, except that on Twitter, everyone who visits your profile can see it. You can see mine at www.twitter.com/Shama. Any graphic designer can create one for you. We create them on occasion as well. Why? It's a great marketing tool, and it will set you apart! You don't get to say a lot using your 160-character bio, but you can make a great impression using your Twitter background. Make sure it includes your name, a way to reach you (email, phone, or both), your major websites, and a brief bio. Keep it clutter free, use your brand colors, and again, be succinct!

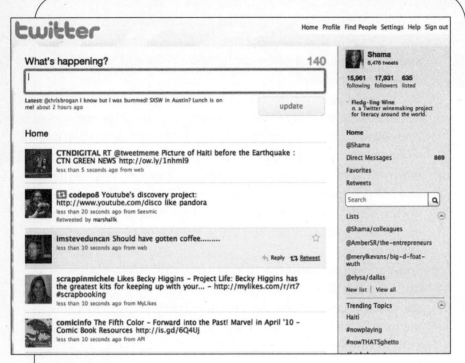

Who to Follow

On Twitter, you can choose to follow everyone you find and amass diverse tweets, or you can choose to follow a specific few from whom you derive value. I follow a variety of people, and it makes for a very robust Twitter experience. If you are interested in someone's tweets, follow him or her. Don't worry about whether he or she follows you back. You will attract your own group of followers.

Here are a few tips to get started:

- Upload your contact list, and see who is already on Twitter. You may be surprised.
- Look for more people you know. Twitter has a search tool that allows you to search for people using keywords and names.
- Feel free to follow me (@Shama). I will follow back. (My open-door policy applies on Twitter as well!)

- If you belong to another social media site, announce that you are now on Twitter. Be sure to give your username. Status updates on Facebook and LinkedIn are a great way to make announcements like this.
- Once you have at least five followers, look at who they follow. If they seem interesting, follow them.
- Use Twellow.com and WeFollow.com, directories of people on Twitter organized by industry and interest. You can look for people to follow and list yourself as well. For example, if you are a PR pro, you'd want to look for reporters so that if they need a source for a story, you are there. Follow people within niches: industry, city, occupation, and so on. It is a great way to meet locals.
- Check to see if your favorite bloggers, actors, or media personalities are on Twitter. Chances are they are. Follow them. Often they are easier to get in touch with via Twitter because it only takes them a few characters to respond.
- See who the people you follow recommend. I often recommend good people to follow. There is a current trend on Twitter called Follow Friday. Twitterers recommend who they follow to their followers followed by the #followfriday or #ff hashtag on Fridays. (You follow?)

Marketing via Twitter represents a very unique and compelling new channel for marketers. Its ease of use, transactional speed, pure text format, and ability to reach a large audience in 140 characters offers simplicity and yet complexity. For big brands, the ability to connect directly with consumers offers a free fall of both good and bad feedback, and many are using Twitter as a customer service channel. Furthermore, for transactional products, a very compelling promotion can get unbelievable reach and offer a potential viral impact. For individuals, social media influence is driven by content and relationships. Many have built strong personal brands with Twitter by sharing and creating content and engaging individuals and companies.

Mike D. Merrill,
MikeMerrill.com

How to Make the Most of Twitter

Think of Twitter as a global human search engine. It is completely what you make of it.

Let me give you an example. I was scheduled to speak to a group of CEOs for a company called Vistage that I had never spoken to before. The group's host had forewarned me that this could be a tough crowd because they often really grilled their speakers. Hearing this, I did a quick search on Twitter for "Vistage Speakers" and found five. Using the @ sign, I asked them if they had any recommendations. Within two minutes, I had a variety of responses like "use statistics and case studies" and "Best of luck! Let us know how it goes." Folks I had never met before—one in China—were wishing me well.

> The main purpose of marketing in any institution is to tell the story behind the brand. How do you connect well with your customers in order to sell your product or service? Twitter is a great tool to use in order to show that "personality" behind a company or a brand. Use Twitter to drive people (traffic) to a blog that tells your story. Talk about your customers, clients, and your business. Twitter is a great avenue to connect with customers on a personal level, as well as on a professional level. Use it to your advantage.
>
> Kyle Lacy,
> *author of* Twitter Marketing for Dummies

This same experience has repeated itself in various areas. When I first got my dog, Snoopy, I had no idea what it was like to raise a puppy. I'd frequently turn to my Twitter followers and ask, "Do puppies eat peanuts?" or, "My puppy sleeps a lot! Is that normal?" I always get excellent answers.

Tom Morris, writer and philosopher, wrote an insightful article called "Twisdom: Twitter Wisdom" for the *Huffington Post* (www. HuffingtonPost.com, Sept. 9, 2009). Morris writes:

Twitter is not mainly about telling the world, or your forty-seven followers, what you had for lunch. And it's not just about Ashton and Oprah, or who can attract the most followers the quickest. It's about building a new form of community. It's about learning. It's about support, inspiration, and daily motivation. And it's also about fun. But the most important aspect of Twitter may be that, if you do things right, you begin to surround yourself with an incredible group of people eager to share their best questions and insights about life. They're all looking for new wisdom and hope. Twisdom is the result.

There's collaborative thinking on Twitter at a level and in a form I've never seen before. Almost every day, and often many times a day, a topic comes up that causes me, as a philosopher and simply a curious individual, to ponder a bit, and then share the results of that pondering in the 140 character increments, or "tweets" that Twitter allows. One comment will spark another, and before long, people of different ages and walks of life from around the world are engaged with me and each other in an extended conversation of brief bursts that add up to new realizations for everyone involved.

Multiple Twitter Accounts

Can you have multiple Twitter accounts? Yes. Should you have multiple accounts? It depends. Some people have an account for business twittering and another for personal twittering. I think this is a difficult balance to maintain, because it is tough enough to get traction going for one Twitter account. However, it can be done. Dave Taylor (www.AskDaveTaylor.com) does a great job with his business account, www.twitter.com/FilmBuzz, and maintains a personal account as well. I have seen others successfully maintain business accounts, offering coupons, monetary deals, and so on. There are also service-oriented accounts that tweet current deals or respond to customer service issues. There are news services that tweet only headlines. You can choose what type of an account you want.

Be careful, though: it needs to be something that people value or enjoy. Dave's business account is successful at least partially because film trivia and reviews are something that people enjoy more often than not.

Following and Unfollowing

We've discussed who you should follow, but can you un-follow someone who isn't providing value? Absolutely. If someone you follow doesn't add value to your life, feel free to stop following him or her. This is not an etiquette issue.

How do you get people to follow you? Try the following.

- Don't answer Twitter's question ("What are you doing?") literally. No one really cares about the fact that you just brushed your teeth or have to go pick up the kids from school, unless you can make it valuable. Avoid saying, "Going to pick up kids." Instead, say, "Picking up kids from school. I-35 and Beltline are jammed. Find another route." That's helpful!
- Leave out mundane details *unless* they add value. Avoid things like, "Loving this veggie burger." Use, "Loving this veggie burger at the new San Francisco joint on 45th and Lemon."
- Share valuable content. If you find a great site or useful tidbit, share. It's also okay to share content that you wrote yourself, as long as it's useful. My company gets 20 percent of our website traffic from Twitter using this method.
- Ask genuine questions, and welcome feedback. While writing this book, I often turned to my Twitter followers and asked what they would like to see addressed. Thoughtful questions can also lead to engaging discussions that can help you better understand others' perspectives and obtain feedback. This is key to building relationships.
- Put a button on your blog or website inviting people to follow you. A huge collection of buttons can be found at www.vincentabry.com/31-logos-et-boutons-pour-twitter-2480 (Note: This website is not in English).

- Make it a point to follow at least two new interesting people per day. They may follow you back!
- Host a contest or giveaway. Many high-profile bloggers have done this. They ask people to follow them and retweet their contest message to enter the contest, so their name is spread quickly. This works if (1) you already have a good following (at least a few hundred), and (2) the giveaway is solid.
- Don't ask people to help you get more followers to reach a certain number. It looks awful. It is okay to ask *if* you have a goal that isn't about your follower number. Avoid saying, "Please help me get to 500 followers. I am so close. Thanks." Instead, try, "I'd love to meet more people in the Detroit area. Can you recommend any?"
- When tweeting links, shorten them using a URL-shortening service. This way you can fit more characters into a single tweet. Also, many URL-shortening services, like www.BudURL.com, www.SnipURL.com, tr.im, and bit.ly, allow you to track how many clicks a link receives. This is a great way to figure out what attracts folks to your website—and then do more of it!

Do the numbers matter? Yes. I wish I could say that they don't, but the number of people who follow you does matter. Why? The more people who follow you, the more reach you have. Today, when I ask a question or need feedback on an idea, I get ten to fifteen replies very quickly—and that's with 17,000 followers. So, yes, numbers matter.

Does this mean that you should obsess over the number of people following you? No. It's still better to focus on a smaller pool of people with whom you have connected rather than thousands with whom you haven't. You want to carefully manage quality as you increase quantity. As more and more people follow you, you can find tools that will help you categorize and organize the tweets. If you use TweetDeck, for example, you can organize your followers into categories. I have mine set up into two rows. The first contains all my followers, and the second is a list of colleagues and personal friends.

A Word on Auto-Following and Automated Direct Messaging

There are many applications out there that will allow you to auto-follow, meaning automatically follow back those who follow you. There are also applications that let you do automated direct messaging, in which you send a canned direct message to all your followers. I don't recommend either technique.

When Twitter was new, automatically following people was a good way to give kudos (if you follow me, I will follow you back) and to grow your network. However, because Twitter has grown so rapidly, it has attracted its share of spammers. Unlike Facebook, which monitors and suspends accounts for even remotely suspicious activity, Twitter takes a more laissez-faire approach in governing. Spammers are notorious for following people who auto-follow and then un-following them. This skews their count so it looks like 10,000 people are following them and they are only following a handful. Can you think of any reason why 10,000 people would follow a spammer? Of course not. This is the whole point of their trick. They make it seem like they are legitimate by taking advantage of those who auto-follow.

Automated direct messaging is also a huge Twitter don't. There was a time when I believed automated messages could work when used properly, but because of Twitter's growth and users' misuse of the function by spammers, I recommend against it.

Using Twitter to Attract, Convert, and Transform

Twitter is one of those rare social networking sites where you can do all three! You can attract people to your website, convert followers into consumers and customers, and transform your past successes by sharing stories and case studies.

Posting links is a great way to attract people to your website. I once wrote a post called "10 Things to Do Immediately After a Networking Event" that included a link to our company blog. It led to 1,125 visits to our company blog when I tweeted it (and others retweeted it). That one article with a link attracted over a thousand people! Of that thousand, many chose to subscribe to the blog, becoming permanent consumers. Some will go on to convert into clients.

There are also times when we find people twittering to search for something—such as web design, SEO, or social media help—in lieu of asking a friend or using a search engine. When we find such folks, we offer—without being pushy—to help them. It's even better when someone who is following us tells them, "Hey, The Marketing Zen Group does that kind of work well. Connect with @Shama." Often that turns them into an instant client for us!

Then, when we do the work, we share our results. For example, I might say, "Just launched a blog for K9Cuisine.com! Check it out here: blog.k9cuisine.com. That was a great project!" Or, we might share a case study or a story. This is difficult to do in 140 characters, but it can be accomplished with some practice. For example: "Client needed to reach a very targeted audience. Set up a Facebook page and targeted group XYZ. Got 800 clicks and a 20% increase in sales."

Twitter Applications

Because Twitter is growing at such a fast pace, applications to bolster it are being created on a daily basis. Here are a few of my favorites:

- TwAitter (www.twaitter.com): TwAitter allows you to schedule your tweets, create groups, manage multiple users, and monitor your brand.
- TweetDeck (www.TweetDeck.com): TweetDeck allows you to manage Twitter on your desktop. It shows you the tweets of people you're following, replies, and direct messages in three clean columns. No clicking back and forth necessary!
- SocialOomph (www.SocialOomph.com): SocialOomph allows you to release tweets in the future. Going on a vacation but found some good content to share? You can use this

application to write tweets ahead of time to post automatically while you're gone.

- SocialToo (www.SocialToo.com): Similar to SocialOomph, SocialToo allows you to filter tweets to avoid spammers and sets up surveys that your Twitter followers can take—a great way to get feedback.
- Mr. Tweet (MrTweet.com): Mr. Tweet is a true personal networking assistant. It recommends people to follow and also tells you who is following you. It's a great tool to help you build your Twitter list.
- HootSuite (HootSuite.com): HootSuite allows you to track multiple accounts and supports multiple users. It also lets you track statistics such as how many people clicked on your last link.
- TwitPic (www.TwitPic.com): TwitPic allows you to share pictures on Twitter. It's very easy to use!
- TweetBeep (TweetBeep.com): TweetBeep allows you to set up email alerts for keywords that you want to follow on Twitter.
- Twitterfeed (Twitterfeed.com): Twitterfeed is a service that feeds your blog to Twitter. Use it in moderation! You don't want your Twitter stream to be full of your own posts.
- BubbleTweet (www.BubbleTweet.com): BubbleTweet allows you to combine video with Twitter. You can create a quick video introduction of yourself using this application and put it on your Twitter profile. The one downside to BubbleTweet is that it gives you an alternative URL. For example, mine is www.bubbletweet.com/id/mgnxe. It plays the video and then turns into my Twitter URL. However, I cannot get it to play directly on my Twitter profile without using a different URL. Despite this drawback, this application is still worth it!

You can see a continually updated list of newly created Twitter applications at www.birdsallsocialmedia.com/2009/04/04/birdsall%E2%80%99s-massive-twitter-sites-tools-directory.

Twitter on Your Phone?

There are a number of applications that also allow you to twitter using your phone. Here are a few:

- Twitterific (Twitterrific.com): Twitterific is a tried-and-true application for the iPhone.
- ÜberTwitter (www.UberTwitter.com): ÜberTwitter is a good tool for using Twitter on your BlackBerry.
- Twidroid (Twidroid.com): This application is the best choice (and one of the few) for the Google T-Mobile Android.
- Twitter Mobile (m.twitter.com): This is Twitter's own mobile site.

Searching Twitter to Join Relevant Conversations

Knowing how to search on Twitter is crucial, because that is how you know which conversations to join! Practicing savvy searching skills on Twitter is like practicing good listening skills in a face-to-face conversation. If you don't search, you won't know who is looking for you—and, perhaps more importantly, who might have a complaint or concern. Complaints and concerns are best addressed publicly so others can see that you are a company that cares and is tuned in. Many big companies such as Comcast, Dell, and JetBlue use Twitter to offer customer service. They search for mentions of their name and engage those users in a useful conversation.

You can search Twitter conversations directly from your Twitter home page. You can also set up keyword alerts (similar to Google alerts) using a service like TweetBeep. What should you search for? Your company name, your personal name, and any industry-related terms. Also, be sure to search for phrases related to the service or product you offer. For example, if you are a web designer, you should search for "need website." This is one of the beautiful things about Twitter. People *often* search for what they need in a very public manner. It is not uncommon to see people asking for referrals and recommendations. *And* it is okay to offer up your product or company in a nonintrusive manner. Recently, I was searching for some project-management software, and I asked for recommendations. Shortly afterward, two owners of project-management software companies asked whether I had seen their site and if I would like a demo. This is a great example of selling made simple. Best of all, because I was looking for this information, I was grateful to hear from them.

The following are three stories on how I have leveraged Twitter to further my own business.

1. **Snagged a speaking engagement:** I follow the founder of a very prestigious blogging conference. I had just submitted my speaking proposal through his website when I sent him a public message giving him a heads-up on the proposed topic. No sooner had I sent out that tweet than a well-known blogger retweeted the message and added something along the lines of "you would be missing out if she didn't present." Almost immediately, I got a direct message from the founder saying he liked the topic and that I was in. It all happened within seconds! Don't underestimate the power of Twitter. Since then, people have often noticed my speaking topics when I tweet and asked me to speak at their events.

2. **Found direct clients:** We get at least two leads a week from Twitter. Someone inevitably sees a tweet about a website we just finished, or a ranking we achieved for a client, and wants to know what we can do for him or her. That is social media at its best, because you are attracting new clients by transforming your old successes into stories—or, in this case, tweets!

3. **Established expertise:** We once had a client who hired us solely by looking at my tweets. He said they were proof that we knew online marketing; our tips on Twitter convinced him. Establishing my expertise has lead to multiple speaking opportunities, more clients, and articles in various

publications. It has also led to some great joint venture relationships. Colleagues who do complementary work will often see what we do and refer their clients to us. It is a win-win situation for all.

Twitter Do's and Don'ts

DO:
- ✓ Use your tweets strategically. Know what you are trying to accomplish with your tweet.
- ✓ Follow people you admire, even if they don't follow you back.
- ✓ Be on the lookout for valuable content to share with your followers.

✓ Treat your followers with respect. There are lots of viewpoints on Twitter, and without nonverbal cues, it's easy to offend people. Use sarcasm with care.
✓ Respond to direct messages and @ replies.
✓ Create a community of colleagues.
✓ Ask genuine questions—you'll get good answers!
✓ Retweet when someone shares something valuable.
✓ Share relevant pictures and videos.
✓ Work on attracting people to your site (using real value, not pushy links).
✓ Share mini-case studies about your successes.
✓ Learn to tell stories in 140 characters.
✓ Track how many people click on your tweeted links

DON'T:
☒ Try to force anyone to follow you. I have seen people get angry because someone won't follow them back. You can only decide who to follow—not who follows you.
☒ Ask someone why they un-followed you. Respect their decision.
☒ Mass-follow people. (Really *look* at who you want to follow. This is your chance to create your own human search engine.)
☒ Post links to only *your* website. (No one likes someone who constantly self-promotes.)
☒ Twitter when sleepy or inebriated.
☒ Ask followers to help you reach a certain number of followers.
☒ Promote something you haven't tried yourself, just to make a few bucks.
☒ Tweet something you wouldn't want someone to find. (Tweets are indexed by Google and can come up in people's search results.)

How to Be Proactive on Twitter

The following tips will help you proactively use Twitter.

- **Get instant market feedback.** When I asked my followers on Twitter which they would prefer—an ebook or a whole course on social media marketing—I immediately got answers and rationales. Twitter is a *great* way to test out your ideas before taking them any further. You do need to have a few hundred followers for this to be a successful test.

- **Show your followers respect.** There are companies out there who will pay you to tweet ads in the form of links. The bigger your follower base, the more you get paid. This is an awful way to monetize on Twitter. I have seen the backlash firsthand when I tested a service called Magpie. It doesn't matter if you actually have used the products you are advertising; people see it as an intrusion.Don't advertise outside products using Twitter.

- **Let people sample your style and work.** If blogs and websites are novels, tweets are short stories. Twitter is a great way to allow people to taste a sample of your work. Tweet tips related to your industry, and let your personality shine through. If you are witty, be witty. If you are known for your warm nature, show that to the world!

- **Generate quality traffic.** You can generate some quality traffic from Twitter, because followers have already sampled your work or style. They may even feel like they already know you! The best traffic is generated when you share a content link from your website and people retweet it.

- **Build trust.** Social media is very much about transparency. The lines between personal and professional are blurred. Twitter is your chance to build trust with future clients and customers just by being yourself! We trust people with whom we come into contact more than we trust strangers.

- **Generate content.** Twitter is the number-one spot to find guest bloggers and interviewees. Have a blog? A podcast? Want to interview someone? Twitter is a great way to reach out to him or her!

- **Generate ideas.** If you just "listen in" on Twitter, you can see immediately that it is a marketplace buzzing with ideas. People are asking questions (that you can potentially provide answers to) and sharing thoughts. There are many movers and shakers on Twitter!

- **Get online PR.** As noted above, bloggers hang out on Twitter a lot. And you know what bloggers have? Communities of followers. Twitter is a great way to make friends with bloggers and reporters. Be genuine. They need stories as much as you need the press.

- **Find people to hire.** There are some very talented folks on Twitter. Whenever we are hiring, we look there first by sending out a tweet letting our followers know we are hiring, and by searching specific phrases such as "web developer + Dallas." We have hired two interns we found on Twitter.

- **Manage your reputation.** Every day I see at least three people or companies being talked about that are not on Twitter and probably don't have a clue as to what is being said about them. Don't be like them. Twitter is a great way to see what people have to say about your service and product. You can also use Twitter as a customer service tool, answering questions and taking queries live. Already give great customer service? Perfect! Use Twitter to make it transparent.
- **Send out your newsletter.** Many newsletter services these days will send out a link to your newsletter through your Twitter account when they send out your newsletter via email. AWeber (www.AWeber.com), MailChimp (www.MailChimp.com), and Blue Sky Factory (www.BlueSkyFactory.com) all have this feature.

LinkedIn
The Place Where Professionals Go

Why Bother with LinkedIn?

- It has 43 million users representing 170 industries.
- It's a network geared toward professionals looking to network—the members are there to talk shop!
- It is excellent for online visibility.
- It's a great way to showcase expertise.
- It serves as the ultimate online Rolodex.

LinkedIn is like a buttoned-down office-networking event. If Facebook is happy hour, LinkedIn is all business, in a suit and tie. It is not my favorite networking site, but I do believe it has enough benefits that you shouldn't dismiss it too quickly when marketing your business. It's especially useful to those in the business-to-business (B2B) sphere.

LinkedIn Basics

LinkedIn is a great way to connect with former bosses, colleagues, and clients. Chances are they are there!

LinkedIn offers both free and paid accounts. A paid account allows you to send InMails (email messages within LinkedIn) to those who are accepting them. This is a good way to reach people who may not currently be in your network. A paid account is not necessary, however, to make the most of LinkedIn.

LinkedIn allows you to give and receive professional recommendations, and you can choose to feature these on your profile. This is an excellent feature to showcase your aptitude and talent. Much of LinkedIn is about creating an interactive résumé for yourself.

Everything you need to know about LinkedIn can be divided into five segments: your profile, managing contacts, LinkedIn answers, LinkedIn groups, and LinkedIn events.

LinkedIn is really your résumé on steroids. The site has a number of advanced applications that allow you to promote your products, services, events, businesses, and brand, and drive targeted traffic to your websites. It also ranks extremely high in Google's search engine, which gives you another platform to promote your name when someone searches for you.

If you want to bring your business or brand to the next level, then it is critical to take action and start optimizing LinkedIn to achieve your goals.

Lewis Howes,
co-author of LinkedWorking

Your LinkedIn Profile

Think of your LinkedIn profile as an interactive online résumé. Your colleagues, prospects, and vendors can all see your professional life in nutshell. Here is a screenshot of the first part of my profile:

Shama (Hyder) Kabani

President of The Marketing Zen Group: A Web Marketing Firm, Social Media Specialist, Speaker/Trainer, Web TV Show Host

Dallas/Fort Worth Area | Marketing and Advertising

Shama Kabani Time Spent on Social Media sites up 82%. Twitter and FB lead the pack. http://bit.ly/73uOPk 2 hours ago from Twitter

Current	• **President** at **The Marketing Zen Group**
Past	• LOA Coach at Divine Reach Coaching • Owner at Private Tutoring and College Prep
Education	• The University of Texas at Austin
Recommendations	**14** people have recommended Shama
Connections	**500+** connections
Websites	• Online Marketing Firm • Online Marketing Blog • Social Media Show
Twitter *NEW*	• Shama
Public Profile	http://www.linkedin.com/in/shamahyder

Use the following tips to create the best LinkedIn profile for yourself.

• Use a good headshot, ideally one that frames your full face and shows you smiling! (You can use the same one across all social media sites.)

- When you receive recommendations from colleagues and clients, showcase them on your profile. When someone posts a recommendation, you will get a message asking you to accept.

Recommendations For Shama

President
The Marketing Zen Group ☐

"Shama is extremely knowledgeable, articulate and personable. Her insight into what is hot on the market and how to position yourself, no matter your field, is priceless." *January 4, 2010*

Top qualities: Great Results, Expert, High Integrity

(1st) Melody Brooke, Marriage & Family Therapist
hired Shama as a Speaker in 2009

"I had the pleasure of hosting Shama at a conference where she discussed how job seekers can use online social media to help them in their search. She was warm and witty, and most of all extremely knowledgeable about the benefits of maintaining an active online presence. If you are looking for advice or consultation in this area, I encourage you to strongly consider Shama." *November 25, 2009*

(1st) Terry Beneke, *Chief Investment Officer, Antares Capital Management*
was with another company when working with Shama at The Marketing Zen Group

"Shama is highly knowledgeable in her field of business and, at the same time, is capable of quickly understanding her clients' business models. She is a delight to work with and understands her clients' needs for having a real bottom dollar effect. I am glad to have found her and now I can outsource several business functions to her without a worry and at a reasonable cost. I highly recommended Shama Hyder." *June 15, 2009*

Top qualities: Great Results, Expert, High Integrity

(1st) Yousef Shaban
hired Shama as a Business Consultant in 2009, and hired Shama more than once

- Your summary is key. Write it to be read. Use adjectives, and make it pack a punch. It's okay if you have to rewrite it a few times. It can (and should) be a work in progress. Here is a screenshot of my current summary:

Summary

Shama Kabani is the President of The Marketing Zen Group, a full service online marketing firm that serves clients around the world. She has been dubbed the "master millennial of the universe" and "an online marketing shaman" by Fast Company. She has aptly been named one of the 10 Most Influential and Powerful Women in Social Media. In 2009, Business Week honored Shama as one of the Top 25 under 25 entrepreneurs in North America.

Shama holds a Masters degree in Organizational Communication from the University of Texas at Austin, and prides herself in being a constant learner. Her website, http://www.MarketingZen.com has turned into a high-traffic destination for people looking for advice on how to successfully market their businesses online. And, companies often look to Shama to guide them when it comes to the vast world of social media marketing. She also hosts a popular web TV show on new media marketing at http://Shama.Tv, and the media regularly call on her to comment on marketing and technology trends. Her first book, The Zen of Social Media Marketing (BenBella Books), is due out in the Spring of 2010.

Specialties

Online Marketing Training and Mentoring, Online Marketing, Social Media Marketing, Outsource Marketing, Web Design and Development, Blog Design and Development, Search Engine Optimization, Professional Speaking, Facebook Marketing

- In your summary, use keywords that make it easy for other people to search for you. Include industry terms as well as layman's terms. For example, the airline industry for the longest time thought everyone was searching for "low airfare" only to discover that most were looking for "cheap tickets."
- Remember to check your spelling. This is a professional networking site, and the rules (though unwritten) are a bit more stringent. Whereas someone may forgive a spelling slipup on Twitter or Facebook, on LinkedIn misspelling a word is comparable to making a spelling error on your résumé.

- The "specialties" area directly beneath your summary allows you to "tag" yourself appropriately. Think about how others may categorize you or search for you. What keywords would you want someone to use to find you? Also, what specifically do you specialize in? You will notice that in my specialties section I include "online marketing" (which is very broad so people can find me under that category) and also "Facebook marketing" (which is a specialty).

- LinkedIn allows you to make your profile public. If you are planning to use LinkedIn as a marketing tool, by all means make it public. This allows search engines to find you as well, making keyword usage even more important.

LinkedIn Tips

Assess whether your audience really uses LinkedIn. It is a great tool for business-to-business social networking but may not be ideal if you sell services and products to individuals and retailers.

Post a provocative and honest profile. Be sure your profile doesn't read like a résumé. Nobody cares how many certificates and awards you have on your wall. They do care what specific results you have helped create for your clients. [You can see Lisa's profile at www.linkedin.com/in/energizegrowth.]

Proceed pragmatically. Don't be seduced by shiny pennies on the floor; be practical and realistic about your strategy. Think about how a specific action, posting, or comment will hurt or help your company. Ask yourself, "Who will manage the content? How do we maintain consistency across all social networks? Would I be okay if this posting showed up on front page of the New York Times, BusinessWeek, or the Economist?"

Visit LinkedIn on a weekly basis. Ask genuine and industry-related questions. This increases your credibility. Recruiters, authors, and potential alliance partners will notice you. [Lisa doubled her LinkedIn community within just a few months by offering valuable resources and knowledge in the LinkedIn answers section. Now, she is approached regularly with requests to be featured in articles, books, and virtual meetings.]

Lisa Nirell,
author of Energize Growth NOW: The Marketing Guide to a Wealthy Company

Managing Contacts

Who should you connect with on LinkedIn?

- Past and current bosses. Especially add those with whom you have a good relationship; they are great folks to get recommendations from.
- Your clients and customers. If you have a huge list of customers, only add those with whom you have connected personally via email or phone. In other words, add only those who would recognize your name!
- Industry contacts such as vendors, distributors, and resellers. Essentially, add all business contacts.
- Bloggers who cover your industry or might cover your product. Not all bloggers will be open to connecting on LinkedIn, but some will.

LinkedIn Answers

LinkedIn's "answers" section is an area where you can ask and answer questions. This is a great way to showcase your expertise. Sometimes companies that use this feature are also looking for referrals. If your company is a fit or what they're looking for, you can definitely approach them. But above all, the LinkedIn answers feature is perfect for two things:

1. **Market research:** I once asked what people wished to learn more about within the field of online marketing. Social media marketing was on top of the list! You can also answer questions that others post. On the next page is a screenshot of some questions asked under the internet marketing category. I can see that someone is curious to know if it is okay to use Twitter to generate leads. By clicking on this question, I can go to a page that shows me the full question and gives me the option to answer it. Or I can answer on my blog and post the reply link to the question. I can then share that same post across my social networks.

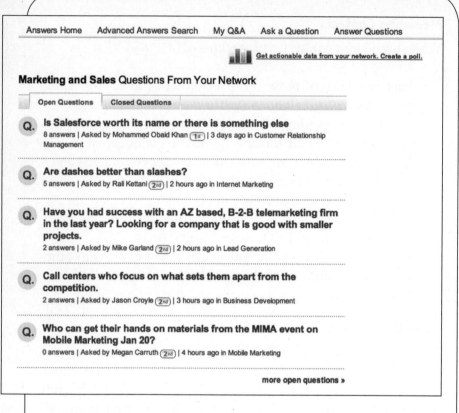

Get actionable data from your network. Create a poll.

Marketing and Sales Questions From Your Network

| Open Questions | Closed Questions |

Q. **Is Salesforce worth its name or there is something else**
8 answers | Asked by Mohammed Obaid Khan (1st) | 3 days ago in Customer Relationship Management

Q. **Are dashes better than slashes?**
5 answers | Asked by Rali Kettani (2nd) | 2 hours ago in Internet Marketing

Q. **Have you had success with an AZ based, B-2-B telemarketing firm in the last year? Looking for a company that is good with smaller projects.**
2 answers | Asked by Mike Garland (2nd) | 2 hours ago in Lead Generation

Q. **Call centers who focus on what sets them apart from the competition.**
2 answers | Asked by Jason Croyle (2nd) | 3 hours ago in Business Development

Q. **Who can get their hands on materials from the MIMA event on Mobile Marketing Jan 20?**
0 answers | Asked by Megan Carruth (2nd) | 4 hours ago in Mobile Marketing

more open questions »

2. **Showcasing expertise:** When a LinkedIn member asks a question, he or she also gets to choose the best answer. LinkedIn uses a rating system to award points to the person whose answer is chosen. This can be showcased on your profile with a badge that says, for example, "Public Relations (5 best answers)." This is a nice boost in credibility when someone is looking at your profile for the first time.

LinkedIn Groups

LinkedIn groups are similar to Facebook groups. They're a great way to find people with similar interests. Once you have joined a group, it will appear on your left-side navigation bar under "Groups." Here are some ways LinkedIn groups can be useful:

- **They let you send InMail to members without having to upgrade.** This feature itself makes LinkedIn groups useful. If you try to message someone who isn't connected to you, LinkedIn will ask you to upgrade. Join a group that that person is a member of, and you can send him or her a message without upgrading. Again, this works best if you have a genuine interest in the group and aren't using this feature as a spam mechanism.
- **They're a great way to communicate with your group or organization online.** Look under the "Discussions" tab on your group page to view current discussions or start your own.

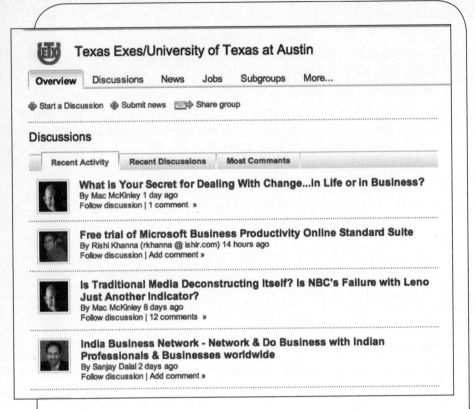

Texas Exes/University of Texas at Austin

Overview | Discussions | News | Jobs | Subgroups | More...

Start a Discussion   Submit news   Share group

Discussions

Recent Activity | Recent Discussions | Most Comments

What is Your Secret for Dealing With Change...in Life or in Business?
By Mac McKinley 1 day ago
Follow discussion | 1 comment »

Free trial of Microsoft Business Productivity Online Standard Suite
By Rishi Khanna (rkhanna @ ishir.com) 14 hours ago
Follow discussion | Add comment »

Is Traditional Media Deconstructing Itself? Is NBC's Failure with Leno Just Another Indicator?
By Mac McKinley 8 days ago
Follow discussion | 12 comments »

India Business Network - Network & Do Business with Indian Professionals & Businesses worldwide
By Sanjay Dalal 2 days ago
Follow discussion | Add comment »

- **Those searching for you can find you more easily.** If someone is searching for a speaker, he or she is likely to find you more easily if you are already part of a LinkedIn speaker's group.

To find groups to join, look through LinkedIn's group directory at www.linkedin.com/groupsDirectory. (You can also find a link to this directory under "Groups" in the left navigation bar of your profile page.) In certain groups, your membership may have to be reviewed by a group manager before you are accepted. For instance, college- or company-related groups may require an email address associated with the college or company. If you have questions about a group, you can send a message to the owner listed on the group information page.

LinkedIn Events

The LinkedIn events feature (shown on the right-hand side of your home page) lets you know about upcoming conferences and industry events. It pulls events from sites such as www.Event-Brite.com and makes recommendations for you based on your industry and the contents of your profile. It also allows you to search for events. It is a great way to see what hot events are occurring in your industry. You can also

see which of your connections on LinkedIn will be attending. It isn't LinkedIn's most exciting feature, but it is one more way you can connect with others.

LinkedIn Do's and Don'ts

For the ultimate do's and don'ts on LinkedIn, I reached out to Jason Alba (CEO of JibberJobber and author of *I'm on Linked-In—Now What???*), Mike O'Neil (CEO of Integrated Alliances), and Viveka von Rosen (Always Extraordinary). I asked all three LinkedIn experts to provide me with unique do's and don'ts that are often overlooked. The first five tips in each list were provided by Jason; the rest were provided by Mike and Viveka.

DO:
- ✓ **Flesh out your profile.** Too many profiles are sparse, with little information. Not only does this decrease your chances of being found when someone is searching for talent, but when someone does find your profile, he or she doesn't have much to go on.

- ✓ **Participate in LinkedIn answers.** This might be the best way to communicate with your contacts, which is critical in nurturing relationships. Use the answers feature to stimulate conversation and gather information.
- ✓ **Join groups.** When you join groups, you have extra privileges with group members that you would only have if you were first-degree contacts. This is also a great way to find people who share like interests without having to find them in search results.
- ✓ **Use the advanced search.** This is a very powerful part of LinkedIn and can help you find contacts you should get in touch with or add to your network. Go beyond the basic search and explore the power of the advanced search.
- ✓ **Export your contacts.** On the Contacts page, toward the bottom, there is an "Export Connections" link. I recommend you do so to create a backup, and also take it a step further: import them into a CRM (customer relationship management) tool. That way you can manage the relationships with more detail without being subject to LinkedIn's restrictions.
- ✓ **Treat your LinkedIn profile like a website.** Make sure it is well-formatted, clean, and, most importantly, of interest to others. Ask friends to read it, and ask them to be very critical in their assessments. This should not be an "attaboy" moment.
- ✓ **Populate your LinkedIn profile with keywords.** The keywords should reflect your background, your industry, and the industries of your *clients* to make it easier for potential clients to find you. Be sure to include the variants of the words (teach, teacher, taught, teaching), the synonyms of those words (speaker, educator), and the variants of *those* words (speaking, education).
- ✓ **Make your page visually interesting.** Look into using special symbols (◊) to break up your text and add emphasis to key elements.

DON'T:

☒ **Don't spam.** Don't come to LinkedIn hoping to hawk your wares. This is a place to network, and business happens here, but people want to focus on relationships, not listen to your next cool pitch. Make sure you are authentic and care about them before you start talking too much about your company or product.

☒ **Don't forget who might see your profile.** Getting too casual or too serious, or not being compelling enough, might cost you in business or opportunities. Have your profile ready for your target audience, and when they find it, you'll have the credibility you need.

☒ **Don't misunderstand the concept of connections.** Will you connect with everyone? What about your competition? Or will you connect with only people you have met in person? Everyone has a different connection strategy appropriate to him or her. You need to figure out your own connection strategy.

☒ **Don't send canned invitations.** When you invite someone, go into the invitation message and customize it. Let him or her know who you are and why you want to connect.

☒ **Don't preach.** I get invitations on LinkedIn telling me all the virtues of LinkedIn. When I see these invitations, I know the senders have not read my profile, and I assume they are just adding me to increase their numbers (as opposed to wanting to develop a relationship with me).

☒ **Don't use anything in your name field that doesn't belong as part of your name.** For example, don't use "Paul A. (Pablo_paul@yahoo.com), PABLO A." when you can use "Pablo Paul," or LinkedIn users will not be able to find you when searching for you by name. This is also a violation of the LinkedIn User Agreement, and you don't want to lose your account.

☒ **Don't put anything in the picture area but a headshot picture of yourself.** No group pictures, no kids, no spouse, no logo. A professional photo is not required; just use a simple headshot picture from any standard digital camera. LinkedIn will help you crop it to the required 85 × 85 pixels.

☒ **Don't use the default descriptors for websites, such as My Company, My Website, and so forth.** Put a custom label in place of this text by selecting the "Other" option from the pull-down menu used to select the descriptor. It pops up a new field so that you can put in a custom label. It is okay to point to specific subpages on a website.

☒ **Don't include only recent jobs, as you may be tempted to do.** Put in all of your work history, back to college days. This gives you more inroads to create more relationships with others.

☒ **Don't use paragraphs longer than five lines as they appear in the View My Profile section.** Break up paragraphs with six or more lines into multiple paragraphs.

AHA! Zen Moment

How should you ACT on LinkedIn?

Attract: Create a compelling profile. Use LinkedIn groups to connect with others who might be good referral sources or potential joint venture partners.

Convert: Use the LinkedIn answers feature to get strangers to consume your information and perhaps even turn into clients!

Transform: Get recommendations from your contacts on LinkedIn. This is a great way to showcase your expertise!

How to Be Proactive on LinkedIn

The following tips will help you proactively use Linked In.

- **Gain more visibility.** By adding connections, you further the likelihood that someone will find you when they need you. Write a compelling profile, and keep your contact database updated with your professional contacts.
- **Increase your rank with search engines.** LinkedIn allows you the option of making your profile public, which will allow search engines to index it. This is a very smart move, because LinkedIn is ranked very highly by search engines. When you create a public profile, select "Full View." Instead of using the default URL LinkedIn provides, customize your public profile's URL to include your actual name.
- **Get business advice.** LinkedIn answers are a great way to get advice and find answers to your most pressing questions. This is an especially useful tool if you are a business-to-business company.
- **Conduct market research.** I have done some excellent market research using the LinkedIn answers feature. Not sure what your potential clients or customers feel their greatest need is? Just ask. Need to test out the market with a new idea? Ask for feedback. LinkedIn's answers feature makes it easy.

> "Spending on online video advertising will grow to $4.6 billion in 2013, representing a more than sevenfold increase from the $587 million spent on the format in 2008."
>
> eMarketer.com

Video:
The Next Frontier

ALTHOUGH VIDEO doesn't usually fall within the category of social networking sites, it is an important tool within the bigger sphere of online marketing. You can take the online video you create and share it across the board from your own blog to social networking sites. If content is king, video is the king of the bigger country.

My number one source for online video information is Dave Kaminski of Web Video University (www.WebVideoUniversity.com). Dave teaches thousands of people online how to create successful online videos through his training programs. He is the expert when it comes to this area, so I have asked him to write this guest chapter.

In February 2005, three men launched a new website. In November 2006, Google bought that website for $1.65 billion. The website was called YouTube. Thus began the phenomenon of web video.

Web video is the fastest-growing form of media in history. Sixty-two percent of internet users (and growing) watch web video regularly. Almost 7 billion videos are viewed each month across Google's network. Over twenty hours of video are uploaded to YouTube every minute. And Cisco predicts that video will drive 80 percent of web traffic within the next four years.

Why is there such a love for web video? In large part it's because that vast majority of people, when given the choice, prefer to watch rather than read. In fact, a 2007 study by the National Endowment for the Arts reports that "on average, Americans aged 15 to 24 spend almost two hours a day watching TV, and only seven minutes of their daily leisure time on reading." And you can bet that web video is only further fueling this difference in time spent watching versus reading across all age groups.

Crafted intelligently, web video is a brilliant viral tool to attract, engage, and convert viewers to take action better than any other marketing medium on the web.

Sherman Hu,
ShermanLive.com

But what does all of this mean for you, the website owner, business owner, blogger, or online marketer? What's the most effective way to use web video for your business? And how can you get started with web video if the technology confounds you? If you've never touched a camera in your life? I share the answers with you here. Answers that aren't based on theory, hearsay, or speculation, but rather on the real-world results of people who are earning their incomes, in full or in part, through web video.

Of course, there are lots of ways you can make web videos: you can record what you're doing on your screen, piece together videos using nothing but photos and stock footage, or turn the camera on yourself and star in your own videos. But whatever you do, you're going to need some tools to create those videos. So to start, we're going to cover equipment and software for web video creation. Then we'll discuss secrets for making people watch your entire video, video sharing sites, video podcasting, making money with web video, and the future of web video.

The Equipment You Need to Create Web Videos

This is often the most boring part of web video. However, it's also the part where people tend to have the most questions. Specifically, they want to know what equipment is the best.

My answer may surprise you. That's because when it comes to video equipment, there is no "best"—no best camera, no best microphone, and no best software. In the world of video, best is really a matter of opinion.

There are, however, certain guidelines you can and should follow—guidelines that will save you plenty of time, money, and headaches. We'll start with video cameras first.

Virtually any video camera you buy these days will produce video that's of high enough quality for the web—even a $150 Flip camera. That doesn't mean you're going to get gorgeous, vibrant, broadcast-quality video—not even close. But your footage will be good enough for the web.

If you want higher quality, you're going to have to spend more on a camera. With video cameras, you truly get what you pay for.

Personally, I use cameras from Canon's VIXIA line. Sony cameras are just as good. In fact, if you were to go out and buy a camera today, I'd recommend you get a model from either Sony or Canon. As a rule, cameras from either of these two manufacturers will give you the best quality with the fewest headaches.

No matter what camera you choose, you'll want to make sure it comes with an external microphone jack. This jack will allow you to plug a microphone into your camera—for example, a lavalier microphone—which you can then attach to the front of your shirt. If you use an external microphone like this, the audio portion of your video will sound dramatically better than if you had used your camera's built-in microphone. In fact, this simple tip alone can dramatically increase the entire production value of your video.

Should You Use High-Definition or Standard-Definition Video?

First, understand that, whether you use HD or SD video, it's still just video. The difference is that HD uses a lot more pixels, which means a sharper and more detailed image.

That better image comes at a price, though. To edit most HD video and get it ready to go on the web, you'll need a powerful computer—one with a multicore processor and at least 4 GB of memory.

That's why, for people just starting out, I recommend sticking with standard-definition video. It's faster and easier to load online and to work with, and you don't need the latest and greatest computer hardware to get things done.

If you have the resources to work with HD video, by all means do it. Ultimately, that's where all video is headed, including video on the web. Just understand that from a business standpoint, there is no advantage or disadvantage to using HD rather than SD video. It's still just video. And the only thing you gain with HD is a nicer-looking image.

No matter what type of format you shoot your videos in, you are still going to have to cut out portions of the video where you make mistakes, or maybe you'll want to add text, graphics, or background music to your videos. To do all of this, you must edit your videos using video editing software.

What You Need to Know About Video Editing Software

There are plenty of video editing software packages available. Windows comes with a free package called Movie Maker. Apple comes with iMovie. There are also inexpensive solutions available from Pinnacle, Ulead, Adobe, and others. But there are only two software packages that I recommend to people: for PC, Sony's Vegas (www.SonyCreativeSoftware.com), and for Mac, Apple's Final Cut (www.Apple.com/FinalCutExpress).

Why these two out of all the options available? Two words: upgrade path.

Both Vegas and Final Cut offer beginner versions on which you can cut your teeth editing video for a low cost. Then, as your skills progress and you start wanting to do more with your video, you can upgrade to more advanced versions of these programs (all the way up to professional versions used to create Hollywood movies and TV shows). And when you do upgrade, you won't need to relearn the software. It's the same software with additional features.

With virtually all other video editing programs available, it's the opposite. They either don't offer an upgrade path or, if they do, they require you to learn a completely new (and confusing) software interface.

But what if you don't want to shoot live video? What if instead you want to record PowerPoint presentations or something you're doing on your computer screen? For this you will need screen recording software.

My Recommendations for Screen Recording Software

First, let's explore the difference between screen recording software and video editing software. Screen recording software allows you to record movement on your computer screen, from demonstrations or tutorials on software to slide-based presentations. Video editing software allows you to take footage from a video camera, stock video clips, or even photos and edit everything in an unlimited number of ways—you're limited only by your imagination. Video editing software cannot record your computer screen. And screen recording software is not designed to edit live footage from a camera.

When it comes to what software should you use if you want to record something on your screen, again, I have two recommendations. For PC, I recommend Camtasia from TechSmith (www.TechSmith.com). For Mac, I recommend ScreenFlow from Telestream (www.Telestream.net).

Although there are multiple competing programs available for each platform, these two are the runaway winners. You cannot go wrong with either of them.

There are also free and inexpensive web-based screen recording solutions available. The most popular are Jing (JingProject.com) and ScreenToaster (www.ScreenToaster.com). These are both free.

Now you know, at least on a basic level, the equipment you should use to create your videos. But that's only part of the battle. You still need to create your videos in such a way that viewers won't get bored and bolt after a few seconds.

Three Secrets for Making Sure People Watch Your Videos from Beginning to End

Many people mistakenly think that simply creating a video and putting it online means that everyone who comes across that video will watch it from start to finish. Unfortunately, statistics paint a far different picture. Here's a look at viewer habits, as reported by the video distribution service TubeMogul:

- Within the first ten seconds of a video, 10.39 percent of viewers are gone.
- Within the first thirty seconds of a video, 33.84 percent of viewers are gone.
- By the one-minute mark of a video, 53.56 percent of viewers are gone.
- By the two-minute mark of a video, 76.29 percent of viewers are gone.

In other words, the web video viewing community has a serious case of attention deficit disorder. To combat that and help hold the viewer's interest from beginning to end, there are three things we can do.

First is to regulate video length. Ideally, you want your web videos to be no more than two minutes in length. When you go beyond that, the number of viewers who click away increases dramatically. This doesn't mean your video has to be exactly two minutes long. However, you do want to keep that two-minute goal in your head. Follow this rule, and the odds of getting your complete message across to people will increase dramatically.

Second is to keep things moving. Watch any TV commercial, TV show, or movie. You'll notice that about every two to three seconds what you're seeing on the screen changes. There will be a different camera angle, a different scene, or a different image shown. And this happens repeatedly throughout the entire program. What you see is constantly moving and changing. We've all watched enough television to have our brains programmed by this. If a scene remains static on the screen for too long—even just ten seconds—we start to get bored and anxious.

In the world of web video, that's when people start clicking away from your video and onto something else. But by keeping things moving (which means avoiding static scenes of ten seconds or more), you help keep viewers interested. It's a subtle but effective trick.

The third (and perhaps most important) technique is transparency—giving your viewer a behind-the-scenes look at your life or business. For example, when web video first started heating up, advertisers repurposed their television commercials for the web. That means they took commercials that had been running on TV and stuck them as-is on the web. The results were disastrous. Turns out people on the web don't want to see TV-style videos. Why? Because the web is a social tool. People use it to connect with others. They don't want to see stiff, contrived, corporate-style presentations; they want to see real people. Which is exactly what transparency gives them.

What Shama does with her videos on Shama.TV is a perfect example of transparency in action. Watch her videos, and you will see that she's not on a fake set or in front of a green screen with a fake background superimposed. Instead, she's at her desk. Or on her couch. Or walking around her neighborhood. Or with her dog, Snoopy. She shares what she's reading, what she learned at a seminar, or even what someone may have sent her in the mail.

The end result is that she comes across not only as a trustworthy authority, but as someone who is genuine, approachable, and real. And that's the idea behind transparency. Use it with video, and both your audience and business will grow.

But, of course, people have to see your videos first. So you need to know how to get traffic and build an audience with web video.

What You Need to Know About Video Sharing Sites

When most people hear the words "web video," they instantly think of YouTube. YouTube, along with Viddler, Vimeo, Veoh, Blip.TV, Dailymotion, Metacafe, Revver, and a host of others, are video sharing sites.

Most people are led to believe that by using video sharing sites, they'll gain a flood of traffic, sudden success, and maybe even instant stardom. Unfortunately, that couldn't be further from the truth. In fact, 53 percent of the videos on YouTube achieve fewer than 500 views, and 30 percent get less than 100 views. So I'll tell it to you straight without mincing any words: posting your videos on video sharing sites should only be used to get ancillary traffic, not primary traffic. There's actually a far, far better way to get traffic with web video, which I discuss later in this section.

First, let's cover how search engines like Google view and index videos. Actually, search engines (for the most part) don't view videos at all. Nearly all web videos are Flash files, and Flash files are more or less invisible to search engines. This means the content of a video isn't being viewed, indexed, and ranked by a search engine, but rather the web page a video is on is viewed, indexed, and ranked. Or, to put it another way, when you upload a video to a sharing site or place a video on your own webpage, search engines know a video is there, but they don't have any idea what that video contains. (Note: This is slowly changing as search engines learn to adapt.)

Search engines do look at the other items on a webpage—blog post titles, page titles, text on the page, incoming links, HTML tags, and so on—and that's how they figure out what a page is about. Again, the actual content in the video is ignored.

So how do you get people to find your videos, and how do you get them to appear in search engines? In the case of video sharing sites, you have to focus on metadata. I know that sounds like a "techie" word, but all it really means is the title, description, and tags you enter when uploading a video.

For example, when you upload a video to YouTube, you are asked to give the video a title, write a description about it, and enter a few tags (words that relate to the video's content). This is your metadata. And what you enter here will determine how your video shows up in search engine results and within the YouTube search results. So when writing your video title, description, and tags, you'll want to target the specific keywords that relate to your video. The image below shows an example of a video upload form with fields for metadata.

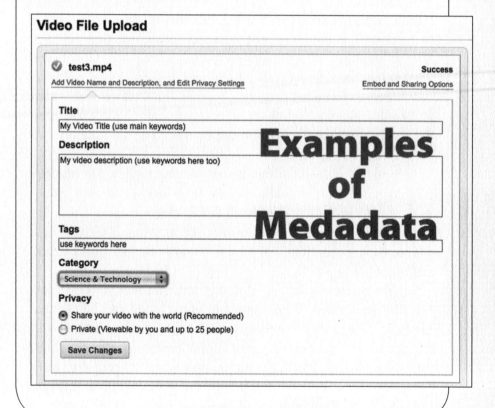

There are also a few services available that will allow you to upload your videos to multiple video sharing sites at once. This means that instead of going to each video sharing site individually and uploading your video, you only have to upload your video once, and it is automatically distributed across multiple sharing sites for you. The most popular of these services is TubeMogul (TubeMogul.com). It also happens to be free. When using a service like TubeMogul, you will be asked to enter metadata for your video, and that metadata will be used for every sharing site Tube-Mogul distributes your video to.

Sounds pretty good, doesn't it? You've got all these free video sharing sites and a free distribution service like TubeMogul. So why in the world would I tell you to use video sharing sites only for ancillary traffic? There are a number of reasons, but I'll highlight the most important.

First, remember that with video, it is the webpage it's on that is being ranked and indexed, not the actual video. And that webpage doesn't belong to you; it belongs to the sharing site. This means your videos are driving traffic to the video sharing site, not your own website. To get to your site, viewers must watch your video and be so compelled by what it contains that they stop everything they are doing and go to your site instead. The vast majority of viewers will not do this.

Second, all video sharing sites are losing money. No one has figured out a way to make money from user-generated video. Even YouTube, which dwarfs all other video sharing sites, has been projected to lose $400 million or more in 2009. (Google acknowledges YouTube is losing money but disputes those numbers.)

What this means for you is that at any moment, a video sharing site can go out of business and close its doors. And if that happens, your videos (and any traffic they may generate) will disappear, too. Just in case you think something like this can't happen, it already has. Multiple smaller video sharing sites have gone out of business completely in the past year. Even Google has announced that they will stop accepting new video uploads to Google Videos, and AOL and MSN have already stopped accepting new videos (though existing videos remain available).

And third, there's a far better way to generate traffic and build an audience through web video. A way that lets you retain total control and ownership of your videos. A way that lets you easily generate top Google rankings for your videos. And a way that allows all the traffic you generate to go directly to your own site. Podcasting.

The Power of Video Podcasting

When you throw around the word "podcast," most people knowingly nod their heads but are secretly baffled by the term. And when you add the word "video," things get even more confusing.

So first let me define what a video podcast is. In technical terms, it's a series of videos released episodically and distributed through RSS. In simpler terms, it's usually a blog that contains all video. These videos focus on a particular topic and contain pure content (no sales pitches). They are delivered once a day, every other day, or once a week. And the built-in RSS feed for the blog can distribute these videos directly to people's email boxes, other websites, and services such as iTunes.

For example, let's say you love to bake, so you start a video podcast on how to bake cookies, cakes, and other treats. One week you create a video on baking apple pie. The next week you create a video on baking chocolate chip cookies. The next week it's cupcakes. And you continue on producing episodic videos like these each week.

Because your videos are on a website you own (again, usually a blog), all the traffic your videos generate goes directly to you. In addition, your video podcast can be picked up, via RSS feed, by multiple podcast directories, which search engines love. Why do search engines love podcast directories? Because they are *authority sites* on the internet. They receive large amounts of traffic;

contain relevant, human-reviewed content; and are awarded high PageRank by Google. For you, this means a video listed in a podcast directory can rank higher in the search engines than the same video on a sharing site.

But it gets better. Your video podcast can also be distributed to huge networks like iTunes, Zune, and Miro. And if that isn't enough, you can *still* take each of your podcast videos and upload them to sharing sites, too, for ancillary traffic.

Though all this usually sounds intriguing to people, they are often still not convinced about this whole podcasting thing. So let me give you some proof. I conducted a head-to-head comparison of a podcasted video and the same video uploaded to YouTube. For this comparison I created a video in which I reviewed the performance of a particular piece of software. This video was posted on my podcast site. The same video was uploaded to YouTube. I used identical metadata for both my podcast site and YouTube. A few days later, I Googled the title of my video. The image below shows the results.

As you can see, both the YouTube video and my podcast site video were listed in the middle of the first page of results, side by side. So we're all even at this point, right? Not exactly.

First, you have to ask yourself if you'd rather have someone click on a link that takes him to YouTube or a link that takes him to your own site. And I think all of us would rather have that traffic go to our own site.

But it gets better. In the next image, you'll see that a podcast directory (Odeo.com) has picked up my video, and it's ninth on the first page of the results.

And if we jump forward to the eleventh entry in the Google results, you'll see my own podcast site listed again.

So going back to our scorecard, if I had uploaded that video only to YouTube, I would have one listing for the video on the first page of Google results, and any traffic that listing generated would have gone directly to YouTube. If I had posted the video only on my podcast site, I would have two listings on the first page of the

Google results and a third on the second page of the Google results. And two out of those three listings will bring traffic directly to my own site.

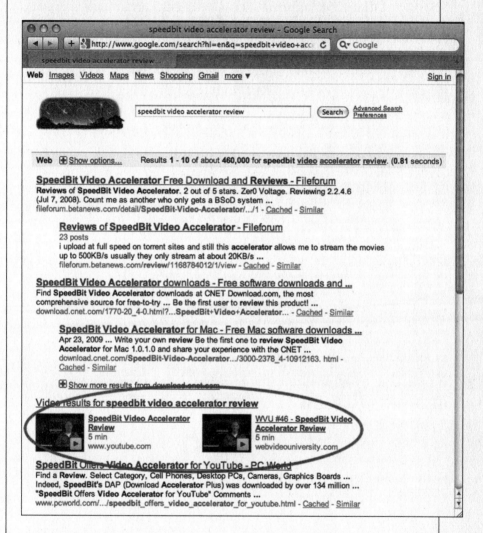

Video results for **speedbit video accelerator review**

SpeedBit Video Accelerator Review
5 min
www.youtube.com

WVU #46 - SpeedBit Video Accelerator Review
5 min
webvideouniversity.com

SpeedBit Offers **Video Accelerator** for YouTube - PC World
Find a **Review**. Select Category, Cell Phones, Desktop PCs, Cameras, Graphics Boards ...
Indeed, **SpeedBit's** DAP (Download **Accelerator** Plus) was downloaded by over 134 million ...
"**SpeedBit** Offers **Video Accelerator** for YouTube" Comments ...
www.pcworld.com/.../speedbit_offers_video_accelerator_for_youtube.html - Cached - Similar

Download **SpeedBit Video Accelerator** 3.0.9.2 - Free **Video** ...
Related software downloads for **SpeedBit Video Accelerator** 3.0.9.2. Related Downloads;
Most Popular; Editor's **Reviews**; New Releases; Latest Technology News ...
www.soft32.com/download_202568.html - Cached - Similar

SpeedBit Video Accelerator 2.2.4.9 review and download. **Video** ...
SpeedBit Video Accelerator 2.2.4.9 review and download. **SpeedBit Video Accelerator**
makes videos from YouTube & +100 sites stream faster.
rbytes.net/software/speedbit-video-accelerator-review/ - Cached - Similar

WVU #46 - **SpeedBit Video Accelerator Review** | Odeo: Search ...
WVU #46 - **SpeedBit Video Accelerator Review** Add this to your Quicklist. WVU #46 -
SpeedBit Video Acceler... July 24, 2009 ...
odeo.com/.../24857348-WVU-46-SpeedBit-Video-Accelerator-Review - Cached - Similar

SpeedBit Video Accelerator Software Informer: version 2.2 information
Review. From the creators of Download **Accelerator** Plus (DAP), pioneers of acceleration
technology, comes a new groundbreaking product! **SpeedBit Video** ...
speedbit-video-accelerator.software.informer.com/2.2/ - Cached - Similar

Searches related to: **speedbit video accelerator review**

speed bit video
accelerator

descargar speedbit
video accelerator

telecharger speedbit
video accelerator

speedbit video
accelerator تحميل

برنامج speedbit video
accelerator

speedbit video
accelerator **firefox**

speedbit video
accelerator **crack**

speedbit video
accelerator **itunes**

Goooooooooogle ►
1 2 3 4 5 6 7 8 9 10   Next

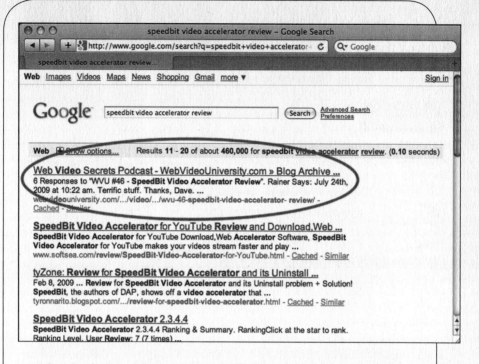

Why do these podcast videos perform so well in the search engines? No one knows for sure about the inner workings of search engines and the complex algorithms they use. However, it's suspected that Google favors both blogs and video content. And with video podcasting, we're using both. In addition, because videos are distributed via RSS feeds, they can instantly appear on multiple websites, which often link back to your website. And the more relevant links you have pointing to your website, the higher your site can rank with the search engines. This means that through video podcasting, we are able to target specific keywords for a market and can often rank higher for those keywords than we would through traditional SEO techniques.

But let's look at a few more examples of the power of video podcasting. For these examples, I went to my own podcast site (WebVideoUniversity.com/podcast) and Shama's podcast site (Shama.TV). I noted a few of the video titles from each and Googled them. Here are the results:

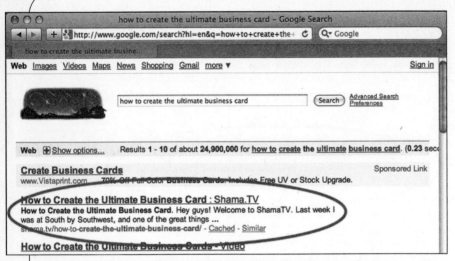

Search phrase: how to create the ultimate business card

Results: 24,900,000

Rank: 1

Search phrase: making MP4 videos play on the web

Results: 1,920,000

Rank: 1, 2, and 3

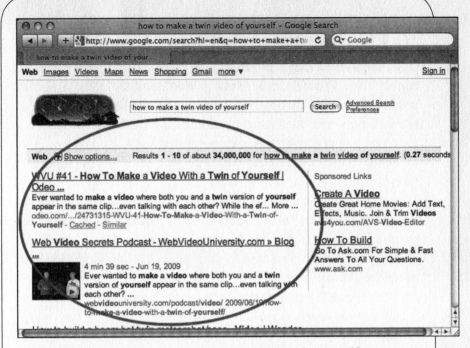

Search phrase: how to make a twin video of yourself
Results: 34,000,000
Rank: 1 and 2

But Are There Any Drawbacks to Doing a Video Podcast?

Yes. Running a video podcast takes passion, commitment, and dedication. You have to continually produce videos on a set schedule (daily, weekly, etc.), and you have to make sure the content is always fresh, relevant, and useful. Do that, and you can achieve the same results that Shama and I and many, many others have.

However, if you roar out of the gate only to give up a month later (which a lot of people do), you obviously won't get the same results, if any. You can still post videos now and then to your site, and you may pick up some rankings for them, but you won't build traffic or an audience nearly as effectively as you can with a video podcast.

Of course, as we discuss in the next section, there are many things you can do with web video beyond just podcasts.

Two of the Most Lucrative Ways to Use Web Video

One lucrative way to use web video is product creation, as in using web video to create products. There are a number of ways you can do this, from screen recordings that demonstrate software to screen recordings that teach a particular topic to live videos that teach or demonstrate a topic to combinations of both. Video has a much higher perceived value than printed material. For example, an ebook that sells for $29 can carry a price of $49 or higher in video form.

Video products can also be a lot faster to create than printed material. Whereas it may take several weeks or months to create printed training materials, that same training in video form often takes just several days. In fact, I've created numerous video products for both myself and clients over a single weekend. In the old days, when everything was 100 percent written, it would have taken me months.

But there's another ancillary benefit of developing web video skills. And it addresses a market that could not be anymore wide open. What's the market? Creating videos for other website owners. I call it *web video consulting*.

There are billions of websites on the internet. Obviously, not all of the sites are business-related, and not all of the website owners want video. But there is a vast market in which sites are business-related, the owners want video, and they want someone to do it for them. The problem is that there are not enough people out there who can provide these services for them. But for those who can, it can be a very lucrative proposition.

For example, the average cost to have a web video professionally shot, edited, and produced is $3,000. That's just for the video. What if the client wants help with video SEO, website design, or marketing? Those are all value-added services that you can provide for additional fees.

The market is definitely out there and waiting if you're willing to go after it. I have students who right now are actively earning the fees I describe. And some even have to turn away work because they are so booked.

The Future of Web Video

There is perhaps an even more compelling reason for developing video skills. Right now when we watch web video either for entertainment or education, we sit down at our computers to do it. But in the not-so-distant future, we will be watching it directly from our TVs, too. In fact, it already has a name: *IPTV*.

Actually, you can already watch web video on your TV; it's just that the technology is a bit limited, confusing, and bulky. But this is changing fast. New televisions are already being manufactured that will automatically play web video.

This means your audience—your clients and prospective clients—will eventually be able to sit on their couches, flip through the web with their remotes, and pull up your videos. And if you do any type of paid-for videos, they'll be able to order those, too, on demand.

It certainly won't happen overnight, but it will happen. And it's expected that this convergence of web video and television will change the way we think of television.

Web Video Levels the Playing Field for the Little Guy

Web video gives any average person the same reach, influence, and opportunities previously enjoyed by only large corporations and media companies. For example, when in spring 2008 United Airlines broke the beloved guitar of a gentleman named Dave Carroll, he tried in vain for nearly a year to get them to make good on his damage claim. He finally became so fed up that he made a music video detailing his experience with United Airlines. It became an overnight sensation, drawing the attention of major news outlets, newspapers, and even CNN. United Airlines not only ended up with egg on their face, but got millions in free advertising—*all negative*. This would not have been possible just three years ago. Like I said, web video has leveled the playing field for the little guy.

Or let's look at television advertising, the holy grail of the advertising world. It's not cheap—well out of the reach of most small-business owners, especially for national spots. And unless you're selling a product through direct response, you have no idea how well your campaign actually performed. With web video, it's an entirely different story. You can reach a global audience at little or no cost. In fact, top video podcasters have hundreds of thousands of people view their videos *every day*. And they know much more about those viewers, from where they came from to what browser they were using.

But here's the bottom line: it's not often that a technology comes along that is accessible to everyone, doable by everyone, and desired by everyone. Web video happens to be all of those things. People want it. They have an insatiable appetite for it. And even someone who has never touched a camera in his or her life has the ability to provide it. The only thing you have to do is pick up a camera and start. Then never quit.

After training thousands of people across the world on how to create, get traffic from, and profit from web video, I call tell you without a doubt that those who find success always follow these principles: they stop thinking about it, they start doing it, and they never quit.

So now it's your turn. And the question you need to ask yourself is this: would you rather look back a year from now and say, "I wish I had," or, "I'm glad I did"?

Creating a Social Media Policy for Your Organization

SO FAR WE HAVE BEEN FOCUSING on how you can personally have a Zen-like experience using social media. But what happens when your employees start tweeting and creating Facebook pages? What happens if they spill company secrets? What happens if they leave—and maybe not on the best of terms? The best action is to take precaution. Having a social media policy in place is akin to setting expectations. If I could sum up this whole chapter, I'd say a social media policy is about being smart and using common sense. And some companies have just that policy! So, you have two choices here. One, you can decide that you will just trust your team to use common sense and be smart about what they put online. It is simple, and lots of companies do use that method. Two, you can create and implement a more precise policy so everyone knows what the rules are. I use words like policy and rules very loosely. I think they can often connote a very strict interpretation, but that is not what I am trying to impress here. Think of policy as suggested guidelines and rules as "how to play smart."

Remember, *having a social media policy in place does not mean that you get to dictate your image. But you do get to interact responsibly in the conversation that dictates your image.* And, you get to help your employees do the same. There are great benefits to today's technology and its widespread use, but there are also some risks, as dictated by Raj Malik of Network Solutions (blog.networksolutions.com/2009/sxsw-follow-up-corporate-social-media-guidelines). As Malik says, unauthorized or inappropriate commentary or posts online can:

- Get the company, and you, into legal trouble with the United States and other government agencies, other companies, customers, or the general public
- Diminish the company's brand name by creating negative publicity for the company, owners, and partners as well as yourself or your team
- Cause damage to the company by releasing nonpublic information or proprietary information
- Cost the company the ability to get patents or undermine its competitive advantage
- Cost you your job at the company

The following are ten steps to creating your own social media policy.

1. **Decide where you stand.** A policy is only as good as the company that implements it. Essentially, the lines are drawn, and you have to take a stand. How far is your company willing to go in the social media sphere? Will you choose to communicate only in reaction to what someone else says? Will you be proactive in engaging the community (consumers and bloggers)? Without an overall attitude about social media, it can be very hard to create a policy. This doesn't have to be a verbal stance, but it should be a part of your company's culture. For example,

Zappos, a very successful online shoe store, encourages all their employees to partake in social media. In fact, 400 out of their 700 employees are on Twitter. Their stance is that everyone jumps in—and then uses his or her own common sense. It seems to be working for them so far!

2. **Determine what constitutes social media.** A blog and LinkedIn may easily be categorized as social media, but what about online video? What about Twitter? What really constitutes social media? You must have your own (preferably written) definition. This is especially true because new websites and tools emerge all the time. My personal definition of social media is any website or medium (including video) that allows for communication in the open. Let's say that you tell your employees to not mention an upcoming merger until you are ready to announce it. However, two employees chat about it with each other via direct messaging on Twitter, and because of a glitch, the message is made public. Did they break a rule, or do direct messages on social media constitute a private forum?

3. **Clarify who owns what.** Does your company have a Facebook page that is handled by the head of HR? What happens when that person leaves? Who owns that page? That content? James C. Roberts III of Global Capital Group Law offers this: "If there is an offer letter or employment contract, it would normally state who owns what (usually the company). Absent that, the law could default to ownership by the company (but depending upon the state). On the other hand, if the company has turned a blind eye to personal use during work hours then it could be attacked. And, it will depend upon the extent to which what is created is based on company property (IP)." (Note: This is not to be construed as legal advice. Please consult with your own attorney for advice specific to your company.) To keep things simple, make sure your employees know what is theirs and what belongs to the company.

4. **Keep confidential information private.** Although other company policies may address the issue of keeping proprietary and personal information confidential, it never hurts to readdress it in terms of social networking. Because of the casual nature of these sites, it is easier to give away key information without realizing it. Even private messages aren't always secure. Each site is has its own fallibilities. It is best to never share any confidential or proprietary information using social media—publicly or privately.

5. **Decide who is responsible.** Although it is important that everyone understands the company's social media policy, it is also important that one person or a team of people be responsible for managing social media efforts. If a customer does make a public complaint, who will answer it? Do they need to forward that to another department? Social media management doesn't automatically fall under the job description of the web developer, PR person, or HR manager. All employees should be encouraged to interact and represent the brand, but there should be one or a few who are proactively handling queries. The best way to find a social media advocate within the company is to seek out the one person or team of people who are most passionate about communicating with customers in such a manner. They may already be doing so without your knowing it. Seek out those people, and train them well.

6. **Dictate the rules of engagement without being a dictator.** It is a fine line to walk—allowing employees the freedom to engage and protecting the company at the same time. However, it can be done. You can't stop employees from communicating using the new mediums, but you can set some ground rules that work for everybody's benefit. Take a look at Intel's social media policy at www.intel.com/sites/sitewide/en_US/social-media.htm. The Emerging Technology Department at the Air Force has created a flowchart of their own

guidelines, which you can view at http://freshspot.typepad.com/.a/6a00d83451f23a69e20105365f0d62970b-popup. You can actually access a database full of social media policies here: http://socialmediagovernance.com/policies.php.

7. **Address taboo topics.** Although your employees probably already exercise good common sense while participating online, it never hurts to clarify specifically what is off limits. Raj Malik of Network Solutions offers this partial list:

- Topics about which the company is involved in litigation or could be in the future (e.g., policy, customer disputes, etc.)
- Nonpublic information of any kind about the company, including, but not limited to, policies and strategy
- Illegal or banned substances and narcotics
- Pornography or other offensive illegal materials
- Defamatory, libelous, offensive, or demeaning material
- Private/personal matters of yourself or others
- Disparaging/threatening comments about or related to anyone
- Personal, sensitive, or confidential information of any kind

8. **Have a system for monitoring the social sphere.** A social media policy doesn't do much good if you don't actually monitor the space where the conversation is happening. There are plenty of free and paid tools to monitor the online space. There are also firms like ours that offer reputation management services.

9. **Make training easily available.** Think win-win. Nobody likes to be bossed around, especially when it comes to his or her own social networking. However, most people are very open to learning about how to better leverage social media sites to further their own careers and brands. Most people who make mistakes online just don't know any

better. If you expect your employees to utilize the social networking tools properly, you must provide training. What they put out there isn't just a reflection of the company; it is also a reflection of them. Make it a win-win for everybody.

10. **Have a crisis plan.** Let's say you have a perfect social media policy in place. What happens if an employee breaches it? What happens if the people you laid off decide to start a Facebook hate group? Or if a disgruntled customer creates a YouTube video (hey, it happened to United Airlines!)? The worst action is inaction. You must act immediately if a crisis occurs. Ignoring it—or, worse, trying to bury it—will only increase the backlash. Ideally, you have already been proactive in your efforts. You have a company blog, you have a Twitter account, and you have some influencers as friends who will vouch for your company. Either way, you will need to take corrective action right away. First, contact the person responsible. Apologize, clarify, and do what you need to do to rectify the mistake. Second, make a public announcement apologizing and clarifying. Also, address steps put into place that will keep such a debacle from occurring again. In social media, transparency is crucial. This is why step 1 is, well, step 1: decide where you stand.

> "You are in the findability department.
> The marketing department is dead."
>
> Todd Defren,
> *principal for SHIFT Communications*

A Final Word on Social Media: Tools for Attracting Even *More* Business

BEFORE WE FINISH UP, I want to give you a few more tools for making the most of social media marketing.

Integrating Your Social Media Efforts

One of the biggest struggles people face in marketing with social media is figuring out how it all ties together. How does social media fit in with online marketing? What does the big picture look like? You want to integrate your social media efforts not only to save time, but to reach even more people than you thought possible. Let's take a look at some ways you can tie in your social media efforts.

Revolve Your Efforts Around Your Website

This is your home base—where all the action should occur. As I've mentioned, you should do everything you can to organize your social media marketing efforts around directing traffic to your website.

However, you can also use your website to let visitors know about what social media sites you're involved with, giving them the chance to keep in touch with you in other ways. Facebook, Twitter, and LinkedIn all provide badges or buttons you can place on your website, which allow visitors to connect with you on these other sites. If you have a graphic designer or are one yourself, you can create your own.

Make It Easy to Share Your Content

If you have a blog or post articles on your website, find a way to enable one-click sharing. The easier it is to share your content, the more likely people will share. You will reach so many more people in this manner by just leveraging your current visitors. Give your visitors an easy way for people to tell their friends. This is why I really like the functionality WordPress provides. It is a blogging platform that you can build your entire website on. If you use WordPress, you can also download the Share-This plug-in, which allows visitors to easily share your content on their social media sites. It can be found at www.ShareThis. com.

Social bookmarking is another way to facilitate sharing. Social bookmarking, in a nutshell, allows visitors to share their bookmarks with each other. There are websites dedicated to facilitating the collection and sharing of bookmarks. This is a great way to attract new visitors to your website. Although there are many such sites out there, here I will focus on the three that I believe have the most potential to drive traffic to your website.

- **StumbleUpon:** StumbleUpon (www.StumbleUpon.com) is a great tool for driving long-term traffic to your website. It is my favorite social bookmarking site, because it drives quality traffic and it helps you discover quality websites. It also tends to bring a good mix of visitors.
- **Digg:** Digg (Digg.com) is a rather famous social bookmarking website, but the traffic you get from it tends to be short-

lived. Think sharp spikes of quick traffic. The audience on Digg is also partial to technology pieces.

- **Delicious:** Delicious (Delicious.com) is simple to use and has a broad audience. If you aren't familiar with social book-marking sites and need a simple way to get started, this is a great site to get started with.

Synchronize Your Status Updates with Ping.fm

Status updates, across all social media sites, are crucial to pre-senting and sculpting your brand. However, updating all of them can be time consuming. The best tool I have found so far for updating all your status updates at once is Ping.fm.

Initially, you have to input your login information from each of your social media sites. This takes a few minutes. Ping.fm then saves all the login information, and the next time you have an important message to send out, you can do so with just one click. You login and post one single update in Ping.fm. Then, that update is automatically sent across the board to all the sites that you gave Ping.fm the login information for.

There may also be search engine-related benefits to setting up Ping.fm that have yet to be fully unearthed. Recently, Ruth Per-ryman of the QB Specialists (www.TheQBSpecialists.com) sent me an email describing the way her business's Google rank shot up after she signed up for Ping.fm. I was definitely intrigued, so I interviewed Ruth.

How did you use Ping.fm to get ranked in Google for your search term?

Nobody really knows what Google uses to rank pages, and, worse, it's thought that their algorithm changes often. But my key search term "QuickBooks enterprise" shot from higher than twenty pages (I gave up looking after that) to page three within about a week of me signing up for Ping.fm and joining all the network sites they link to. I believe the links to my website from those social networking sites is the reason for the huge increase, because I didn't make any other changes during that period. We're also on the second page of Yahoo, and on the fifth page of MSN/Live now, but I can't honestly say I knew what the ranking was before, because I never checked. But I believe it's very likely they were also twenty or more pages in. We're tinkering with the website more now to see if we can replicate it. For instance, my staff is also signing up for Ping.fm. If we continue to climb up the page ranks, it'll be almost certain that this is the cause.

What is your Ping.fm strategy?

One of my friends told me about Ping.fm a few weeks back, and it sounded like a great way to manage Twitter-type messages and status updates. But I'm the anal sort (good to be when you're an accountant), so one rainy Sunday I went in and added all their networking sites that I didn't belong to. I posted my picture, added my website, and entered little bios. It never entered my mind that it might increase my ranking. But for the last six months, I've been just checking Google to see if I was in the top twenty yet, only to be denied week after week, and then, lo and behold, less than a week after I joined all those networking sites, I was suddenly on the third page. You could've knocked me over with a feather! In fact, when I saw I was also on the third page for Yahoo, I couldn't help but yell—wait for it—"Yahoo!" Great name, by the way; very appropriate.

If you could share one tip or strategy with others looking to do the same, what would it be?

Carve out a day—a cold, rainy day over a weekend is perfect; after all, what else are you going to do?—and just start at the top of Ping.fm's list of networking sites. Join them, and complete your profiles. At the very least, put in your business name and website. It's actually a nifty little tool—you enter one 140-character post, and it'll send your post to all the microblogging and status update sites automatically (you can change your defaults

> The easiest part of social media measurement is simply counting the numbers. Website visitors, blog links, Twitter mentions, and Facebook fans are all numbers worth measuring.
>
> Unfortunately, the numbers only tell us half of the story. Next you need to measure the sentiment of each of these social media channels. What percentage is positive versus negative? Are your efforts pushing that sentiment needle in a positive direction?
>
> Lastly, you need to connect this all to your bottom line. You know you increased the number of mentions on Twitter, and you know that the majority of tweets were positive, but do you know how many new sales were generated as a result?
>
> Understand this trifecta of social media measurement and you'll see success.
>
> **Andy Beal,**
> *founder of Trackur (www.Trackur.com) and co-author of* Radically Transparent

so it only goes to the ones you choose). That's actually what I originally meant to use it for; the surge in page ranking was an unexpected yet delightful surprise.

Since my company, The Marketing Zen Group, already ranks high for many of our top keywords, I have not yet tested this strategy. However, just claiming your personal name and your business name on various social media sites is a good strategy in itself. And if it does result in extra benefits, as in Ruth's case, even better!

How to Measure Your Efforts

Social media metrics is the technical term for measuring your social media marketing efforts. And, yes, this could also be a book in itself. Albert Einstein once said, "Everything that can be counted does not necessarily count; everything that counts cannot necessarily be counted." So much of social media is about building relationships and leveraging word of mouth. How do you measure good will? Sometimes a consumer has to hear about you ten times before he or she will buy. You engage consumers using multiple channels, so how you do know which straw broke the camel's back?

There are some things you can measure—and you should! The following are some straightforward metrics that you can use to start measuring right away.

- **Your bottom line:** I am always surprised by how many people don't at least measure their bottom line. By bottom line I mean how much money you're making. How much revenue is coming in compared to how much was coming in before you started using social media?

  Social media marketing is complex, and it is sometimes almost impossible to track exactly how and why someone came to buy from you. This is because, if done correctly, social media marketing is like filling a piggy bank, each coin bringing you a bit closer to your goal. Eventually, one last coin will fill the jar; however, each coin got you a little bit closer.

  When we ask how new clients heard of us, we often get answers like, "I saw you speak once and subscribed to your newsletter. Then I befriended you on Facebook. However, I had to unsubscribe for a while, because I was busy with other things. Then I saw a status update you made on Facebook to a post you wrote, and it was exactly the help I needed." Do you get the picture? Many coins, one piggy bank. Measure your bottom line!

- **Number of leads:** This is another very straightforward metric. How many leads did you get before you implemented social media marketing, and how many leads do you get after?

- **Website visits:** Currently, Twitter is responsible for 20 percent of our company's website traffic. We use Google Analytics (a free tool provided by Google) to measure how many people visited our website and where they came from.

- **Sales cycle:** Measure how long it takes to make a sale to a new client. If your best friend was selling you a car that you needed, how long would you hesitate before buying? Given that you had the money and trusted your friend, not long! Compare that to buying a car from a dealer. How many dealers would you visit? How much research would you do? Social media marketing allows you to be that friend—the person or company that people trust.

  For instance, when prospective clients come to our company, they are often already ready to buy. And these aren't small purchases. On average, a single account is worth $30,000 to $40,000. They just have a few questions. We don't submit long drawn-out proposals or go back and forth proving that we can do the job. They already know we can, because they have seen us online. They have visited our website, seen us on Twitter, and perhaps even seen some of my videos on Shama.TV. If you can establish your expertise online, you will find that people are more than eager to do business with you.

- **Conversion rate:** Let's say that before doing any social media marketing, one out of ten people who came to your website bought something. After you follow all the directions in this book, two out of ten people are buying. Your conversion rate just went up! Why might this be? People are more comfortable buying from brands they trust. While you may not be Coca-Cola, you can certainly establish trust through open communication and transparency. I am more willing to buy from someone I know I can get in touch with easily than from a no-name online. What about you?

Wrap-Up

To wrap up, I want to leave you with three main points to take away:

1. **Strategize first.** Before you create a single profile or partake in a single online conversation, map out your overall online strategy. What will you use to attract? What will you use to convert? What will you use to transform? The tools you use to do these things will be your tactics.
2. **Be human.** Remember that behind every Twitter name or Facebook profile is a real live human being. The ultimate goal is to always connect with that person. Even if you're talking to a group, that group comprises individuals who crave personal connection and attention.
3. **Have patience.** Measure your social media efforts, but also have patience. Social media marketing is a long-term strategy; pay attention to the results you're getting as you go, but always keep your eye on the horizon.

By now, I hope you have a much better grasp of social media marketing and what it entails. I further hope you have realized that leveraging social media isn't hard; you just have to know how to use it, and it can be an incredibly powerful tool. It is truly the Zen way of achieving success!

> "Sometimes the questions are complicated and the answers are simple."
>
> Dr. Seuss

Burning Questions and Answers: Taking Questions and Dishing Out Answers and Advice

WHEN I WROTE THIS, I wanted to make sure I covered the topic of social media marketing in the most comprehensive and useful manner I could. To that end, I asked my blog readers to ask me their most pressing questions. Although most of their questions have already been covered in a general way in the previous chapters, I wanted to include some direct, specific answers as well. Because these questions come up often, I hope the answers will benefit you, too!

Q1: *Within the last decade, we've seen many technology trends come and go. In your opinion, why will social media marketing stand the test of time, outside of its being an exciting, dynamic, and ever-evolving way to market?*

A1: I don't know what social media will look like in another hundred years. I can say with much confidence that it will be here for many years to come. It may take on a different form, but its essence will not change. By essence I mean that people now know what it is like to have their own microphone—to have their opinions heard. You can't change that. You can't push and bully people anymore. People *will* talk, and today their messages can reach thousands. You want to leverage this power for the better, and that isn't going away anytime soon!

Q2: *Is social media marketing meant for all audiences? Is there a group for which it isn't a good fit?*

A2: The chances that your buyers aren't online are slim. Even if you serve geriatric patients, I can bet their caregivers still look for information on the internet. *How* they use social media can differ greatly. Do they just read articles but not interact? Or do they like having their own say? Which sites they use can also vary. For this, you will have to research your audience. Two books I *highly* recommend reading on this subject are *Meatball Sundae* by Seth Godin and *Groundswell* by Charlene Li and Josh Bernoff. If you are marketing to baby boomers, *Dot Boom* by David Weigelt and Jonathan Boehman is also a fantastic read.

Q3: *Is it better to focus on traditional or social media?*

A3: It depends, because the meaning of "traditional media" is changing. For example, it is quite common now for newspapers to have an online edition. Some are even focusing more on their online versions, and still others provide only online versions. I recently heard that email marketing is now considered traditional. Traditional marketing itself is evolving to encompass more and more. In the end, your focus should be on whatever medium allows you to reach your audience.

Q4: *How do I find truly qualified prospects online? I seem to always run around with circles of friends or peers. I find my colleagues more than prospects.*

A4: This is not an uncommon situation. It is easy to end up in the same circles, especially when your colleagues (and competitors) are also early adopters and use social media. The best way to expand your circle is to use Facebook groups to meet new people. You can even create your own Facebook group. If you use Twitter, you can search for people with similar interests or problems (that you can solve!). This is also why it is important to drive people to your website and collect their information there. They may not belong to your circle, but they may run into your website. Find a way to stay in touch with them.

Q5: *I get so many invites for Facebook applications! It spins my head. Do I say yes to all?*

A5: On the contrary, feel free to say no—liberally! Only say yes to applications and groups that resonate with your professional mission. Many applications force you to select at least seven friends to use the application yourself; it's one of the reasons you get so many application invites. Just say no! If you choose to just stick to the Facebook basics outlined in Chapter 4, you will be doing more than fine!

Q6: *If you have a new follower on Twitter, is it okay to invite him or her to join you on other networks? What is the proper etiquette here?*

A6: Yes, it is okay to invite people to join your other networks. *But* you shouldn't bombard them with requests or let this be your only communication with them. It's a good idea to get to know them first. Ask them what they do, and share information about yourself; build at *least* an acquaintance relationship. Otherwise, it looks like you are just trying to rack up your numbers, and no one likes being just a number.

Q7: *How do I find the time to interact with social media to really connect with people without spending all my time doing it?*

A7: First, find two social media networks to focus on. Then, come up with an online networking strategy that works for you. This doesn't have to be complex; it can consist of simple tasks. Let's look at a *simple* Facebook networking strategy: log on, update your status, wish your friends a happy birthday, respond to your messages, pick one person from your network to get to know better, and set up a call with him or her for the week. Fairly simple, right? It can be easy to lose track of time on social media sites, so you can even try setting up a timer. Once your thirty minutes are up, you are done! This does require some discipline on your part.

Q8: *What should you do if someone wants to be your friend on Facebook, but he does not tell you how he knows you or why he wants to be your friend? Is there a downside to accepting him as your friend if you don't know him?*

A8: This depends on your friending policy. I know some people who will only befriend those they know offline. Others will befriend anyone and everyone. You have to find the strategy that works for you. If you are planning to use Facebook as a way to meet new people, then you may want to consider accepting friendship requests from strangers. In my case, I reach more people through my blog and work than I meet personally. I have a wide audience, so I have an open-door Facebook policy. Anyone can befriend me. However, I am *just* as quick with my "Remove from Friends" link (which can be found at the bottom left of a Facebook profile). If a "friend" spams me or sends me too many inane requests, I remove him or her. So, in a nutshell, my Facebook friending policy (much like my policy in life) is friend until proven otherwise.

Q9: *Does social media marketing work well for multilevel marketing businesses? I feel like my industry isn't trusted.*

A9: My experience is that social media marketing works for any type of business, but you have to figure out a way to add value to your network. Multilevel marketing schemes are an extremely misunderstood business model because of companies that ruined the industry's reputation. Social media is a great way to educate people, and you can use that to improve the way people think about multilevel marketing. Does this take time? Yes. Does it work eventually? Absolutely.

Q10: *How do you weave social media marketing with offline marketing?*

A10: Anytime I speak or attend an offline networking event, I come back with loads of business cards. Instead of sticking them into a Rolodex, I search for the people on Facebook and LinkedIn. I add them there and throw away the cards. This way I even know their birthdays! That's one strategy. Aside from speaking and networking, I don't do much marketing offline.

Q11: *What do you do when someone you know through your personal life posts messages on your business social media profile that don't match up with your business life?*

A11: Great question! It depends. If the message is generic or speaks to me as an individual, I don't mind it. For example, my cousins often leave "we miss you" messages on my Wall. I am okay with this. This doesn't make me less professional in other people's eyes. In fact, it humanizes me even more. On the other hand, if I receive an inappropriate message from a personal friend, I quickly delete it. If it was just a silly link, I don't say anything to her. I just delete. If I feel like she may not be up-to-date on Facebook etiquette, I delete her post and then message her privately, asking that in the future she contact me privately instead.

Q12: *Why do we use war terminology ("campaign," "tactics," "strategy," "target") to refer to social media as if the people we're reaching out to are our enemies, to be attacked, pillaged, and plundered?*

A12: Good point. I am not a fan of the violent connotations either. This started because traditional marketing's view of consumers was much harsher than today's view. In the earlier days, you had to *make* someone get your message. You had to convince and convert. Today, the best strategy is to present potential customers with value and choices. It's a game changer. Unfortunately, the vocabulary has stuck, because it's what we are familiar with. If I used "approach" instead of "strategy," it might confuse some readers. Not all, but some. My goal is to communicate to be understood. For now, that involves using familiar (albeit not the friendliest) vocabulary.

Q13: *How do marketers reach business owners who say that they have no time for social media? Or those that feel social media in general is a time vampire?*

A13: Give them a copy of this book. Better yet, tell them that people are social creatures (news flash) and that people are *already* talking about their businesses online. They can either be part of the conversation or not. This is a choice every business has to make. As a marketer, you can help them strategize, give them tools, and show them how to measure. The results should speak for themselves.

Q14: *How many social networking groups should someone be in?*

A14: Focus your strategy and networking efforts on a few sites at a time. Ideally, you should focus on two social networking sites and go deep. Understand the rules, cultivate relationships, and get comfortable using them for business. My experience is that most people who join smaller or niche social sites are already part of the bigger ones. It is rare to find someone joining a new social network as an early adopter who isn't already part of a bigger one like Facebook or LinkedIn.

Q15: *When supplying content to your social sites, should you repeat the same articles and blogs, or do rewrites with completely fresh material?*

A15: Share what you currently have. There is no penalty in repeating information; you don't need fresh content for each social networking site. For example, Facebook allows you to import your blog posts and turn them into Notes. This is a great way to propagate your information. That being said, I don't recommend repeating yourself too much. You want to share your information without seeming like an automated machine. You want to focus on sharing the same information across several media channels, not repeating the same message on one like a robot.

Q16: *How do you know which social media site gives the best ROI on your time and effort? Do I join each new one that pops up, or do I lurk, listen, and take my time?*

A16: Lurk, listen, and take your time. Don't join every network that comes your way. My recommendations are Facebook, Twitter, and LinkedIn. You can also search for specialized social networking sites that your specific audience uses.

Q17: *Any specific marketing tips for the current tough economic times?*

A17: As someone who bootstrapped my company to success, my recommendation will always be the same. Focus on marketing techniques that provide a high return on investment—like online marketing, which costs little and does a lot. Let your current clients and well-wishers be your advertising team. Encourage and reward them for sharing with their friends. Most importantly, stay optimistic. The economic tide is always changing, but people will also always have needs and wants. The only difference in a downturn is that they get extra picky. You have to educate and encourage more than you push. My friends always tease me that my favorite word to use is "leverage." But it is exactly what you have to do in this economy to succeed—and what social media allows you to do with so much ease. Leverage your past success, leverage your well-wishers, and leverage your colleagues by partnering with them. Leverage social media overall to amplify your message and credibility.

Social Media Marketing Case Studies: Regular Folks, Great Stories

SOCIAL MEDIA PROFILE 1:
Yvonne DiVita, Lip-sticking
(www.Lipsticking.com)

In what ways have you utilized social media sites? If you feel blogging is the cornerstone of these efforts, do you think someone can utilize these sites without having a blog?

My foray into social media was via my blog on marketing to women. It opened the door to new and exciting relationships. I met business professionals from all over the world and even from my own backyard. I was able (and still am able) to promote myself, and my business, by sharing expertise and insight, instead of selling. After the popularity of the blog brought me speaking engagements and even client referrals, I branched out into Facebook and Twitter and some other social networking sites that I have been invited to join, such as SWOM (Society for Word of Mouth) and TwitterMoms, as well as Savvy Auntie. I find them useful in building and maintaining great relationships. And I'm able to help other women learn how to market themselves on the web. This brings me recognition as an expert in my field.

I recommend a blog. Can you make a go of it without a blog? I don't think so. A blog is the sincere, personal side of yourself and your business. The blog gives the writer an outstanding opportunity to communicate value and advice without being preachy or sales-y. On the blog, it's possible to engage numerous people in many different conversations, thereby growing your reach and connection throughout the nation and the world. With other networking sites and Twitter, you can initiate the conversation and even share select parts of it. But it all goes back to the blog, where the real opportunity to be yourself exists. Business blogging is extremely helpful for new businesses, as long as the writer remembers to focus on the business and not on too much family stuff. Be professional. If you want to have a blog for family newsletter content, start a family blog.

Which has been your favorite social media site so far and why?

I'm still a blogger at heart. I *love* Twitter. It really has extended my reach and introduced me to hundreds of new people who I can tap into if I need an answer to a simple business question or if I need content to substantiate something I am writing about in my blog. But in the end, I prefer blogs to anything else.

Do you have a social media marketing strategy?

Absolutely! If you're in business, you should never engage in social media without a strategy! Mine is to give thoughtful content and advice, and receive some in return. It's a people-policy kind of strategy—I am here to support people in their business endeavors. It's not about the tools ever! It's about the people.

Anything I can do to be more personal and focused on results for others makes my work worthwhile and successful.

If you could share one tip or strategy with others looking to do the same, what would it be?

My tip would be to always remember your beginnings. In the beginning of our business ventures, we are all eager to talk to experts and take in their advice. Those experts who give freely (always maintaining a level of free advice but gently letting others know that beyond that line is paid consulting) get the best results. Be selective of those you might become a mentor to—it's a wonderful way to give back, but depending on whom you choose to mentor, the time involvement could get away from you.

I'd like to remind everyone that social media is just that: a type of connection that's social. Be sociable. Be approachable. Learn good time-management skills, and understand that no one expects the world from you. Just be the person you wished someone had been for you back when you were getting started. Do this online, via social media tools and networks, and do it offline in a true face-to-face manner. Building your business by learning how to utilize social media, and how to bring it offline in a face-to-face group gathering, will bring you the success you endeavor to achieve. I recently wrote a blog post that quoted Shirley Chisholm, the first African American woman elected to Congress (quoting Arthur Ashe): "From what we get, we can make a living. What we give, however, makes a life."

SOCIAL MEDIA PROFILE 2:
Sandra De Freitas, WordPress Blogsites
(WordPressBlogsites.com)

In what ways have you utilized social media sites?

I use social media sites to automate a lot of my marketing. So, for instance, I enter my marketing message in Twitter, which then updates my Facebook status. To update my Facebook status with my Twitter "tweet," I installed the "Twitter" application in Facebook. To install it you just log in to your Facebook account, and then go to apps.facebook.com/twitter and click "Allow." You then enter your Twitter ID and password and click the "Allow Twitter to Update Your Facebook Status," and you are done!

My tweets are displayed on the sidebar of my blog sites (websites built on a blogging platform), and anytime I publish a new blog post, a new tweet is created, letting people know I posted a new blog post. To do this, I use a fabulous plug-in by Alex King. It's called "Twitter Tools," and it's available at alexking.org/projects/wordpress/readme?project=twitter-tools. I installed this plug-in on my sites and my clients' sites. All I do is enter my Twitter ID and password and change a few of the default settings, and I'm done.

Also, when I publish a newsletter, Twitter is notified, and a new tweet is created in Twitter. This is a fabulous service offered by AWeber. So if you are using AWeber for your email marketing, all you need to do is enable the RSS feed when creating a new newsletter and once again enter your Twitter ID and password. When you publish a newsletter, a tweet is created. Example: "My Newsletter http://aweber.com/b/f2RG."

I have also used social media to make connections with "celebrities" in the industry who otherwise felt out of reach. I start by following them and replying to some of their tweets. They may not follow me right away, or at all, but connecting with them in this way gives me visibility and the opportunity to show them who I am and what I do and give them a bit of my hilarious personality!

Which has been your favorite social media site so far and why?

Twitter by far! It's my favorite on a business level, because I can quickly connect and socialize with potential clients and joint venture partners. It's quite easy to see one's personality and authenticity through tweets, so it helps me filter who I want to work with and who I do not want to work with. On a social level, I love Twitter because it allows me to be social with others at any time of the day or night. I used to love the social conversations my coworkers would have at the coffeemaker, and now Twitter gives me the ability to have that social "coffee talk" virtually.

Do you have a social media marketing strategy?

Yes. Let your personality shine through, and if you don't have a personality, borrow one—just kidding! No one wants to be friends with someone on Facebook who overwhelms their Facebook inbox with invitations to events that are not relevant to them. No one wants to follow someone on Twitter who tweets about gross or boring stuff. I don't want to know that you just cleaned up after your dog; instead tell me something funny like your dog is your employee of the month because he encourages you to have breaks and reminds you to laugh at yourself when you send an email and forget to add the attachment. Tell me about the great new gadget you are using that has made you tons of cashola that month.

Using social media is like publishing a never-ending newsletter. Don't only send me promo stuff, but give me valuable, useful information so I can see you as the expert in your field and I have a reason to refer others to you. The bottom line is to give valuable, relevant, and useful information to establish yourself as the expert.

If you could share one tip or strategy with others looking to do the same, what would it be?

Automate your social media tasks. Twitter can update your Facebook status. Twitter can update the sidebar on your site. WordPress blog posts can be tweeted with a link back to your post. Your whole blog posts can be automated into a Facebook Note. If you use AWeber, then your newsletters can be tweeted on Twitter automatically for you. The list goes on and on!

Barbara Safani, Career Solvers

(CareerSolvers.com)

In what ways have you utilized social media sites?

I used Facebook to reach out to my high school classmates. The idea caught on, and other members of the school started reaching out to classmates as well. The group currently boasts several hundred members. One former classmate reached out to me to create her bio for a new website she was launching, and another contacted me to write her résumé. Both projects resulted in endorsements on LinkedIn and MerchantCircle and additional referrals. I have used Twitter to connect with the media, and as a result, I have been quoted in a syndicated column. I am also using Twitter to drive readers to my blog and my website. On LinkedIn I have used the answers feature to position myself as an expert and to ask recruiters specific questions that job seekers want to know the answers to. I used their responses as the basis for several blog posts. I also use LinkedIn for clients who ask for references. This has speeded up the sales process significantly.

Which has been your favorite social media site so far and why?

Facebook. It feels like you are sitting around the living room chatting it up with your friends, colleagues, and clients. It feels like the most natural medium to me and the platform that is the most fun.

Do you have a social media marketing strategy?

I use LinkedIn to establish industry relevance, promote my brand, and position myself as an expert in my field. I use Facebook to share career information and post events. I use Twitter to share important tips and links to articles and posts with my audience. I also use it to follow my competitors and thought leaders in the careers and social media space.

If you could share one tip or strategy with others looking to do the same, what would it be?

Understand that being on a social media platform requires a certain amount of transparency, and that's not a bad thing. Sometimes it makes sense to bridge the divide between your personal and professional life. When people can see another side of you, you become more real, more trustworthy, and more credible. Letting people in to your personal life (within reason) can help build your brand and help you close more sales or foster more meaningful relationships. Social media is not just a fad. Everyone should take ownership of his or her online identity, because eventually someone is going to Google you. Put your best foot forward, and manage your online presence by creating tasteful and branded profiles on the key social media sites.

SOCIAL MEDIA PROFILE 4:
Craig Drollett, Bin Ends
(www.BinEndsWine.com)

In what ways have you utilized social media sites?

We're constantly changing and upgrading what we focus on for social tools. We use Twitter for our monthly online tastings and have developed our own site, www.TwitterTasteLive. com, as direct access to our program. We are active on Facebook as well and have recently begun video postings using the alpha of 12seconds.tv; we're currently exploring additional enhancements to both sites (www.binendswine.com and www. twittertastelive.com) that will create a much more interactive experience for our users.

Which has been your favorite social media site so far and why?

We have built the foundation of our networks on Twitter because we find that we are able to reach out to more people than with any other platform. With a quick 140-character post, we are able to reach thousands of people, literally, all over the world. Twitter and www.TwitterTasteLive.com (our online wine tasting/social media monthly series) are always the top two referrers to www.BinEndsWine.com.

Do you have a social media marketing strategy?

The issue a lot of people have with web 2.0 is not with basic use and integration but with fully understanding how to use it to disseminate a specific message. You have to adopt the lifestyle, understand why the people following you are actually following you, and understand what exactly they're hoping to get from their interaction with you. If you're constantly selling or broadcasting but not listening or interacting intelligently, then you will get tuned out. Setting up the social networks and integrating them into your own network is not a hard thing to do. The vast majority of what we use is open source and simple to integrate and upgrade. We built Twitter Taste Live based off of the Ning.com social platform. However, the ongoing project took our web design team at Saltline Studio only two days to launch.

If you could share one tip or strategy with others looking to do the same, what would it be?

Be patient, and be willing to adapt to what your users want. Don't sell, sell, sell; just get your message out, and over time you will be found.

SOCIAL MEDIA PROFILE 5:
Shel Horowitz, Principled Profit
(www.PrincipledProfit.com)

In what ways have you utilized social media sites?

To do the following:

- Build my reputation
- Build my network and develop friendships with people
- Turn some of those friendships into new income streams, speaking opportunities, etc.
- Share resources I've found (so much easier to post a tweet than go through the Digg or StumbleUpon process)
- Explore resources others have found
- Find opportunities to get covered in the media, to speak, and to pitch for work
- Vastly increase the reach of my blog by feeding it into Facebook and Plaxo
- Meet others working at the intersections between social change and marketing

Which has been your favorite social media site so far and why?

Twitter! I'm a recent convert, and I'm just amazed how easy it is to connect with people, how much useful information is exchanged, how fast my network is growing, and how helpful people are. But I find as my network grows, I miss far more than I see. I typically check three or four times a day and look two or three screens back. But now, a screen fills up in three to five minutes.

Do you have a social media marketing strategy?

More overall guiding principles: to be helpful; to put up strong content; to avoid catfights; to keep a good balance of personal, business, political, and self-promotional and to not waste my time following people who get way off on this balance; to keep trivia to a minimum; and to include some reference for context when necessary.

If you could share one tip or strategy with others looking to do the same, what would it be?

Be authentic and helpful!

SOCIAL MEDIA PROFILE 6:
Tina Su, Think Simple Now
(ThinkSimpleNow.com)

In what ways have you utilized social media sites?

I've used social media sites to expose my web content to new and existing readers. Some tips I've found useful when utilizing these sites:

- **Make many mutual friends.** Especially ones who share similar interests to those expressed on your site. Get their email addresses, and communicate with them outside of social media sites.
- **Contribute something useful to the community.** And not just spamming the site with links from your domain. Share resources and content that you've found interesting, inspiring, or useful.
- **Be personable and actively participate.** Answer emails, questions, and requests.
- **Help others.** One of my favorite sayings is, "To get what you want, help others get what they want first." It's true. Genuinely and actively help other bloggers promote their stuff; when you have something great published, they'll likely want to help you, too.

I've had great results so far. I've spent zero dollars on advertising and solely promote my site, ThinkSimpleNow.com, through social media channels. Within the first three months, the site exceeded 2,000 subscribers. Within a year, the site grew to 10,000 subscribers and 300,000 monthly page views. I am also able to earn a full-time income through the website.

Which has been your favorite social media site so far and why?
In the following order:

1. **StumbleUpon:** You can quickly gain traffic from just a few people sharing a link for your site. I also love the community on SU; people are passionate about their favorite categories. You can also consistently find useful and original content.
2. **Digg:** On the rare occasion that one of my articles hits the front page, the surge in traffic is phenomenal. It's not the traffic that I seek but the exposure that leads to new potential readers that makes Digg special.
3. **Facebook:** It gives you the opportunity to connect with people on a more personal level and follow what they're up to.
4. **Twitter:** You can easily spread useful links to many people. It's a casual and low-friction way to connect with people— even internet "celebrities."

Do you have a social media marketing strategy?

Meet and connect with as many bloggers and social media enthusiasts as possible.

If you could share one tip or strategy with others looking to do the same, what would it be?

Produce interesting, value-packed, and easy-to-understand content or services. Make it worth someone's time and attention. All these social media strategies can get you some traffic temporarily, but if you don't have the content or product to capture their attention, it's a waste of your efforts.

SOCIAL MEDIA PROFILE 7:
Claire Carton, Carton Consulting

In what ways have you utilized social media sites?

My firm is Carton Consulting; the client is Goucher College. The specific program I promoted for them was the master's in cultural sustainability—a totally new program on a totally new topic and the only one of its kind in the United States.

On Facebook, I created a group for the program and networked with people interested in the topic; I also did paid ads (which were very successful).

I created a blog for the program by the program director. This initiated a number of conversations and showed an upward trend on BlogPulse, as it drove traffic to their home page. Mentions by other bloggers helped also.

I define social media rather broadly; I don't think there's value in separating unpaid online PR from "social marketing." We did a lot of directory listings online, and they drove traffic; also idealist.org was a huge help for us, both in the unpaid listing and their fairs.

Which has been your favorite social media site so far and why?

I would say Facebook has driven the most awareness and response. But the campaign has been so integrated—traffic really did "aggregate" from a huge number of places. Ten people here, ten people there can add up fast if you have hit the targets everywhere they live.

Do you have a social media marketing strategy?

Yes. It begins with understanding the target market to a T: defining the very specific niche you're going after. Then, research, research, research: Where is this audience online? What is their behavior? Only then can you come up with a social marketing plan. You also have to keep an open mind. People defining "social marketing" so narrowly and badly—they don't understand what it is. Essentially, it's a public relations activity that requires a lot of manual labor and content development. Focusing that effort on the places where people spend their time (and it may *not* be a social "networking" site) is still social marketing. "Smart targeting" is the only way to go.

If you could share one tip or strategy with others looking to do the same, what would it be?

Don't apply the same set of sites or media to every singly client or program or product. You really have to be smart and targeted. If you don't understand your audience, you will fail.

Philosophically, I think people are short-sighted about social marketing. The program I outlined here—which involved not only Facebook and the like but also included blogs, directories, forums, press releases, radio, marketing our experts, real content development, offline activities, and so on—was tremendously successful. We saw incremental increases in traffic to our home and apply pages of 300 to 500 percent *per month*. "Integrated" may be a passé concept now, but it's still true. You can't expect magic with "social networking"—there's too much noise. A really great campaign like this approaches the problem the same way traditional media planning always has: by hitting the target with focused messages in a number of media and building frequency and reach over time, and *not* being closed-minded or trying to hit the "next big thing."

SOCIAL MEDIA PROFILE 8:
Chris Geier, K2
(www.K2.com)

In what ways have you utilized social media sites?

We started our entry into social media with a basic "forums and blogs" site. We had to start somewhere, and this seemed a logical step. The goal was to simply give people a place to go and ask questions, and hopefully get answers. Our hope was that we could take this simple act of socializing a problem and grow it into a vibrant interactive community utilizing a broader effort through various forms.

Once we filled a solid need with the community site, we wanted to plan out our next step. Our next effort was to establish a presence in what we saw were the three pillars of social media. Based on additional research, we also found this to be where a fair number of our "community" spent time as well.

1. LinkedIn
2. Facebook
3. Twitter

LinkedIn has a good network of people as well as active groups and discussions. We utilize LinkedIn as a way to engage in the conversation occurring about our field of expertise (Workflow and BPM). We also maintain a corporate profile to better allow people to find us and get basic information on who we are no matter where they look (e.g., Facebook, LinkedIn, Twitter, Google, etc.).

Facebook we are still experimenting with, working to figure out what works best. We initially saw a good deal of interaction and traffic on Facebook when we started engaging there. We have pages and groups created for two of our three products and use them to post basic information and news. We also use them to share event information and let people know what we are up to and how to get involved with us in some way.

Twitter has been the most versatile tool for us. We have used it extensively. Several of us have joined up and regularly interact with the community. I personally also am constantly searching out people who have questions about K2 and/or questions about related topics such as SharePoint, Workflow, BPM, and so on. If I see people asking questions about one of our products or struggling, I try to help, and I also let them know we are here if they have feedback and/or any issues. The main goal here is just to give people another avenue to interact with us. It is very important to us that we ensure if someone has a question or has feedback that he or she has a channel to voice that, regardless of time, place, format, or medium.

Which has been your favorite social media site so far and why?

My favorite social media site thus far has been Twitter. I have found it to be the most versatile and interactive. I am regularly able to interact with K2 customers and partners. We have also been very successful in expanding our community in other ways. We are regularly able to not only get feedback from our community, but also keep them informed and help link/network them together. This helps to grow our community and make it more interactive.

Do you have a social media marketing strategy?

We have a few guiding principles in social media.

1. **Open as many channels to our community as possible.** This will enable as many people in our community to interact with us in a way that is most comfortable and easy for them.
2. **Be part of the conversation.** We need to get out there and join into the discussions that are going on about

not only our product but also our industry and related genres. Doing so not only helps make people aware of us, but also allows us to expand our community and help raise the interaction levels.

3. **Make all conversations open and bidirectional.** Truly look for the interaction and not just take opportunities to broadcast.

4. **Be authentic.** Do not try to hide negative information, but rather let people see it, and then let them see how you fix it.

5. **Manage the intent.** Our intent in social media is to interact and be there for people. Ensure that all decisions made map to that.

If you could share one tip or strategy with others looking to do the same, what would it be?

The primary component of any social media effort surrounds intent and authenticity. To be truly successful, a company must take a step back and understand why they are engaging in a social media effort and then must authentically follow that intent. Not being true in this effort will eventually be seen as fraudulent and greatly damage your reputation and hinder your ability to openly interact with those you seek out. I believe that to be most effective in this genre, you must be in it for the right reasons. You must be in it for the customer and to help him or her in some way. The relationship that exists between a person or entity and others in the social network must be bidirectional; both parties must benefit for it to be effective. I see too many companies out there looking to broadcast and just push information out rather than looking to truly interact and listen. They often say they are there to listen, but their true intent is often unveiled at some point.

I highly recommend before anyone ventures out there and starts talking to people through social media that he or she listen first. Get a better understanding for who people are, where they are, and what they are saying. Then seek to be part of the conversation.

SOCIAL MEDIA PROFILE 9:
Heather Whaling, Costa DeVault
(CostaDeVault.com)

In what ways have you utilized social media sites?

In December 2008, Costa DeVault partnered with the Coalition for the Homeless of Central Florida to add social media to its already strong public relations and marketing efforts. Costa DeVault assisted with initial research, listening, and strategy development. The Coalition focused on five primary goals:

1. Increase online brand recognition.
2. Reach a new demographic.
3. Increase communication, and create a dialog with donors, volunteers, advocates, and stakeholders.
4. Position the Coalition as an authority on homelessness.
5. Encourage active involvement with the Coalition.

Per the recommendations in the plan, the Coalition created a blog, as well as Facebook and Twitter accounts. (They also established YouTube and Flickr accounts, which are in use but are not as active.) Next, the organization identified a staff person who would be responsible for monitoring and participating in social networks—in addition to her existing PR and marketing responsibilities. Specifically, her mission was to participate in social networks to connect with local residents and businesses.

Which has been your favorite social media site so far and why?

The combination of Facebook, Twitter, and the blog have worked well for the Coalition. One by itself wouldn't be nearly as effective. The Coalition has been able to leverage the interplay between the three networks and the Coalition's existing website, each of which reaches a different audience, providing opportunities to repurpose content. Instead of reinventing the wheel, a blog post can be shared on Twitter and Facebook. Likewise, a Flickr album can be posted to all three networks. By understanding how the sites complement each other, the Coalition has been able to extend their social media efforts to three networks without generating three times the work.

Do you have a social media marketing strategy?

Yes! Costa DeVault and the Coalition are firm believers in taking a strategic approach to social media. After all, you need to be able to justify that time spent on Twitter or blogging is a good use of resources. For the Coalition, that meant establishing measurable objectives, such as "increase web traffic by 10 percent," "be mentioned on outside blog posts at least twelve times per year," and "obtain bulk donations of specific in-kind items at least three times a year from social media 'asks.'"

To ensure their efforts aligned with their objectives, the Coalition began the process with research. Before participating in any online conversations, the Coalition took the time to understand which networks are most used by the people they're trying to reach. In addition, the Coalition listened to conversations already taking place to familiarize themselves with each network's subculture—a key part to social media success.

After the research phase, the Coalition laid the groundwork for their own social media efforts, created employee guidelines for social media participation, created profiles on targeted sites, and began to add content and participate in discussions. Evaluation is a key component to their social media engagement. Is their network growing? Are people engaging and interacting with the content they create? Is traffic to their website increasing? Is the network strong enough to make in-kind donations?

If you could share one tip or strategy with others looking to do the same, what would it be?

Many nonprofits and businesses don't have the resources to create an entire "social media department." Instead, they need to integrate social media into their current responsibilities. A tip to make that more manageable: Instead of creating a profile on every network, begin by engaging just a few. Get the hang of those, become a valued member of the network, and then think about expanding your presence. The Coalition chose Facebook, Twitter, and blogging because they align with their overall goals. Yes, you need to monitor keywords on other networks, but that doesn't mean you need to maintain an active presence everywhere. For most organizations, that's just not realistic.

The Coalition can provide a litany of statistics to illustrate the value of their social media efforts—including Twitter followers; Facebook fans; blog traffic, which continues to increase every month; and inbound links. But the most effective way to demonstrate the value of social media isn't in these metrics. Social media matters to the Coalition because when they needed extra help, their online network—people who were strangers just months ago—stepped up to the plate.

The economic turbulence led to a drastic drop in food donations from individuals and in the food supplies available from local food banks. To help meet the shortage facing the Coalition, they decided to test the strength of their online network by launching a bold challenge to the local community: the "Orlando 'Can' Care Challenge." This social-media-driven food drive was promoted via Twitter, Facebook, and the organization's blog.

During the week-long challenge, the Coalition tweeted and Facebooked updates as new donations were brought in and posted photos to Flickr of each donation or group. By the end of the week, with only a few hours of staff time invested in the project, the Coalition was surprised to learn that their network produced 1,000 pounds of food.

That's just one example that illustrates why the time spent building and cultivating an online network is time well spent for the Coalition for the Homeless.

SOCIAL MEDIA PROFILE 10:

Father Chris Terhes,
Romanian Greek-Catholic Association

(RoGca.org)

In what ways have you utilized social media sites?

We used the social media websites to find and get in touch with the proper people who could become sympathetic to our cause and help us bringing awareness about the discrimination and persecution of the Greek-Catholic minority in Romania.

Our activity is a little bit different from that of most of the nonprofit organizations in the United States; therefore I would like to briefly describe what we do so that you can better understand why and how we used the social media websites.

The Romanian Greek-Catholic Association, of which I am president, supports the Greek-Catholic minority in Romania, which is currently facing a cultural and religious cleansing. In 1948 the Communist regime abolished the Greek-Catholic Church in Romania and persecuted its bishops, priests, and believers for their religious views. After the fall of communism in Romania in 1989, despite the fact that our Church was recognized again by the government, the discrimination and persecution continued, hundreds of thousands of Greek-Catholic believers continuing to have their rights violated. Along with the pressure on our people, the Romanian government started a national campaign to destroy the Greek-Catholic heritage, tens of our churches being demolished or destroyed in the last two decades. The U.S. Department of State reported these violations and abuses against our community in many reports during the years.

The main challenge that we had was the fact that most Americans didn't know anything about these abuses taking place in Romania; therefore, the first thing that we did was to build a website to expose this situation. The website was optimized for search engines, and we used many of the techniques related to search engine marketing in order to get more exposure to our website and have it well ranked for certain keywords that were related to our cause.

Our first approach after the launch of the website was to use the regular media to expose the situation in Romania. We sent a press release out using one of the media wire websites. We also sent the press release directly to the main newspapers in the United States, but the exposure was very limited.

Considering the amount that we paid to distribute the press release versus the return in coverage, we soon realized that this is not the path to go if we want to help our community in Romania. We learned from experience (and out of our own pocket) that in the long term, it is better to build a relationship with somebody who writes about a subject related to our cause and make that person aware this way about the situation in Romania than to just spam him or her with press releases. This is the moment when we switched the strategy and we started using the social media websites to find and get in touch with people who could become supportive of our cause.

We started using LinkedIn, Facebook, and Twitter to find journalists, bloggers, or any other type of writers who were writing about religious affairs, foreign affairs, human rights, or any other domain that was connected somehow to our cause.

Using this approach, we were able to find and get in touch with a lot of writers; many of them asked for more details about the situation in Romania, and some of them even wrote a piece or republished our press releases. This was a great chance for me to establish a personal relationship with many of them. We had many of them assisting us with advice or even helping us writing press releases. One of them recently started her own radio talk show and invited me for an interview by the end of September. Without the social media websites, I don't think we would've been able to find so many people supportive of our cause.

Which has been your favorite social media site so far and why?

In our case, the social media website that helped us the most was LinkedIn.

We were using Facebook and Twitter as well, but LinkedIn was by far the best website to find and get in touch with people who could help our cause.

We had a very specific group of people that we initially targeted, and LinkedIn offered us the best solution to find them.

I was amazed by the search options provided by LinkedIn as well as by the search results. Because there are so many search options, you can target your search very well. Also, the groups on LinkedIn offer you a very good chance to know experts and to follow discussions from certain fields. The Q&A option on LinkedIn offers you the chance to get advice from some of the best experts out there. I myself posted few questions on LinkedIn, and I was amazed by how many people offered their expertise on the issue that I addressed.

If you really want to get in touch with professionals and learn from them, I would strongly recommend LinkedIn.

Do you have a social media marketing strategy?

I would rather say that I have certain rules that I follow instead of a defined social media marketing strategy. Because of the rapid changes in the technology, web applications, and new tactics that are discovered for how to use these new web applications, it is very hard to write a strategy in stone. Here are a few of the rules that I follow:

- **Objective.** Before you start planning anything, you have to decide exactly what your goal or objective that you want to achieve is.
- **Know the appropriate tactics that you can use or afford to achieve your objective.** If you have enough money, you can hire a PR firm to take care of everything for you. If you

don't, then you have to identify from the tactics available out there those that you can use or afford to accomplish your objective. For example, you can send a press release to all the journalists in the United States using one of the newswire services available online, but it will cost you a few thousand dollars. This tactic might be very effective for your cause, but can you afford it?

- **Planning.** Once you've defined the clear objective and identified the tactics that you can use, you have to create a plan or a strategy for how to use these tactics to achieve your goal.
- **Execution.** Put your plan in action.
- **Stay informed.** Try to stay up-to-date with news related to social media marketing. New tactics can be developed in this field that you were not aware of when you started your campaign.
- **Be flexible.** Learn from your own mistakes, and adjust your plan. This might include adjusting the tactics that you use, either because you realized that one of them is not working or because a new one was developed, or changing your objective because you realized that it is unachievable.

If you could share one tip or strategy with others looking to do the same, what would it be?

Before you start your campaign, find out the story behind the campaigns that were successful as well as those that failed. It is better to learn from somebody else's mistake than from yours.

Social networking means interacting with people virtually. But like when you interact with people face-to-face, the other person can react in a different way from what you expected. Keep your good manners, and don't take it personally; just move forward.

SOCIAL MEDIA PROFILE 11:
Karen Maunu, Love Without Boundaries
(www.LoveWithoutBoundaries.com)

In what ways have you utilized social media sites?

We started by using a blog to tell the stories of the kids. Telling the stories of the children is so important, because it shows the true difference that is being made. In December 2008, our website was hacked into, and for a while we were without a website. We were still receiving children who needed care—some who needed emergency surgery—that we could no longer raise funds for. Someone told us about the Facebook Giving Challenge sponsored by the Case Foundation that was through Facebook Causes. We are all moms, and none of us had a Facebook page at that time, but our kids did. We braved this brand new world of social media to see if there would be any way we could compete in this contest. It didn't take long before we were helping to sign up all of our friends, family, and anyone else who would help. To win the contest, you had to make at least a $10 donation for your vote to be counted. There was a daily contest of the most unique donations, and each day you could win $1,000 (we won thirteen times), and then over the whole contest period (fifty days), the most unique voters would win $50,000—and we won! We had so many people helping—college students going up and down dorm floors, nurses who brought their computers to work, people who sat in Starbucks trying to get voters. We had a slogan: for $10 you can save 10 lives. In China, a heart surgery is $5,000, so winning $50,000 meant we could heal ten children—and we did.

This was the start of our social media success. We are now using our Cause page to update people on the children we are helping, and we get donations almost on a daily basis. We also have over 14,000 people following us. We feel that since we were already an online virtual foundation, it really helped us to mobilize people to be able to help with getting people to help.

We post stories of the kids on our Facebook Cause page and also on our own FB pages. Our stories become viral in that once a story or a photo is posted, many other volunteers or supporters will post it on their pages, too. Social media has become larger than just one person posting; it has become a community of people spreading our stories.

The success on Facebook has helped us to launch into other sites, too. We are also using Twitter and LinkedIn. Twitter has also been very successful for us, allowing us to personally connect with people and tell our story.

Which has been your favorite social media site so far and why?

Facebook, because we are able to actively get donations from our supporters and share the stories of our kids. From this, our stories are spread all over—so many more people are learning about what LWB does by each of us posting in addition to our Cause page. It is a great place for people to stay updated on what we are doing.

Do you have a social media marketing strategy?

Love Without Boundaries has been well known in the Chinese adoption community, and our goal for social media has been to break outside of this group and to have more people know about our work. When we started branching outside the adoption world, our goal was try to get as many people as possible to learn about our work. We wanted people to see how hard we work and to learn about how this virtual worldwide foundation of over 150 volunteers from 12 countries and 36 states is able to help more than 1,500 children a year. We knew that if people could just hear about us, they would want to learn more and help. It is working! We also want to educate people on adoption and let people know how to adopt. So far, at least one family I talked to on Twitter is in the process of adopting.

Love Without Boundaries is an almost all-volunteer foundation. To keep our overhead the very lowest possible, we don't have an office. We all work out of our homes. Social media has become an extension of how we were already working—online. The Facebook staff and the Case Foundation were shocked that a small charity of moms was able to win against the "big" charities. The reason that we were able to was because we already did so much work online.

If you could share one tip or strategy with others looking to do the same, what would it be?

The one tip that we would offer is to be genuine, honest, and transparent. When people can see who you really are, they will join in and start to spread your message, too. It is like a large bandwagon that others start hopping on, and with this, your message starts spreading far and wide.

Lauren Fischer, NEED Magazine
(NEEDMagazine.com)

In what ways have you utilized social media sites?

When I first came to *NEED* magazine, a little over a year ago, the publication didn't really have a social media presence. *NEED*'s blog and website were updated daily, but there were no social media platforms to promote the stories. We decided to start a Twitter account (@needmagazine) and a Facebook page. We're currently creating a more formal social media platform with Justmeans to reach socially minded businesses. Being a photography-based magazine, we also have accounts with numerous photo sites (Flickr, PBase, etc.). We use all of these sites to further and promote conversation with our readers. We also cross-post *NEED* blogs, other humanitarian stories, and office news.

Which has been your favorite social media site so far and why?

I really like using Facebook because I am able to track what "fans" like and dislike and even respond to the fans who comment on our page. In addition to the content that I post, our fans are also able to upload their own photos, videos, and links. This level of interaction makes Facebook more valuable to me and *NEED*.

Do you have a social media marketing strategy?

NEED's strategy is to keep the conversation alive every day, while staying true to *NEED*'s style and voice. We don't want our social media platforms to become static. The reason why we gain fans/followers/RTs every day is because we're actively updating content. Another aspect of our strategy is to be genuine and have a sense of personality. We don't want to only twitter

NEED blogs and news. Every so often I will comment on a current event, explain an office meeting, or ask others what they think of a recent humanitarian development.

We're a small company, but I'm proud of the social media work I've accomplished at *NEED*. At times I feel silly because it can feel like no one is really paying attention, but then I'll be at a *NEED* event and I'll ask someone how he or she heard about it, and most of the time, he or she will say Facebook or Twitter. Being able to bring people together to support an even greater cause (humanitarian efforts) makes social media 100 percent worth it.

If you could share one tip or strategy with others looking to do the same, what would it be?

Be genuine, and don't forget to interact with your readers/customers/clients. Social media is not just for promoting yourself; it's about communication with your audience. The reason people are following you is because they appreciate what you do. If you return the appreciation, they'll feel even more connected to you and your company.

About the Author

SHAMA HYDER KABANI is the president of The Marketing Zen Group (previously known as Click To Client), a full-service web marketing agency that serves clients around the world. She has been dubbed "an online marketing shaman" and "a millennial master of the universe" by Fast Company.com. Her latest honor comes from *BusinessWeek*, which tagged her as one of North America's Top 25 Under 25 entrepreneurs.

She holds a master's degree in organizational communication from the University of Texas at Austin.

Her websites, MarketingZen.com and Shama.TV, have become high-traffic destinations for people looking to succeed online. Companies of all sizes and the media often look to Shama to guide them when it comes to the vast world of social media marketing. She is an in-demand speaker and has been named one of the 10 Most Influential and Powerful Women in Social Media by Ron Hudson's Immediate Influence blog (based on Alexa Rankings).

Shama resides in Dallas with her family, which includes her husband, Arshil, her dog, Snoopy, and her cat, Maui. *The Zen of Social Media Marketing* is Shama's first book.

You can reach Shama:

> By email: Shama@MarketingZen.com
> On Facebook: www.Facebook.com/ShamaKabani
> On Twitter: www.Twitter.com/Shama
> On LinkedIn: www.LinkedIn.com/in/ShamaHyder

To access the living version of
The Zen of Social Media Marketing
online—with continuously updated
content, video extras, MP3s,
and more—go to:

www.ZenofSocialMedia.com

and enter the passphrase:
thank you